EMPOWERED

Other books in this series:

HEALED

*Stories of women who have
been healed by Jesus Christ*

Compiled by Pat King

JESUS IS LORD

*Testimonies of women who
have experienced Jesus'
power in their lives.*

Compiled by Eadie Goodboy

EMPOWERED

Women's Aglow Fellowship
Lynnwood, Washington

Bible quotations are taken from the King James Version except where otherwise indicated: TLB (The Living Bible), TAB (The Amplified Bible).

Contents

✓ Is That All There Is To Life?. . . . . *Reber class* 11
    By Fran Lance

Life's Deepening Glow of Joy 17
    By Genevieve Miller

The Lord Is My Shepherd. 21
    By Claire Lasher

Faith, Not Feeling 29
    By Pat King

Daddy Never Said, "I Love You!". 33
    By Jerry Witt

Miracles — By the Power of His Spirit 37
    By Shura Temoschenko

Frosting On The Cake 41
    By Ethel Jones

Ours For The Asking 45
    By Betty Denham

How Good To Be Free!. 51
    By Dorothy Boyd as told to Quin Sherrer

Why I Pray In The Spirit 55
    By Jo Anne Sekowsky

Great Is God's Love 59
    By Alice Wikene

Happiness Is The Lord 63
    By Lee Perry

His Love Overflowing. 67
    By Alice Brown

Love, Or Else! 73
    By Martha Banks

Second Chance From God 79
    By Rita Reed Bennett

Adventure Unlimited 87
    By Sister Augustine

Introduction

I first noticed Tina during the closing minutes of a prayer meeting at St. Luke's Episcopal Church in Seattle. A "street" child, she probably was an attractive girl, but it was hard to tell. Her long, uncombed blonde hair half covered her face; her clothes spoke of Salvation Army bins.

Two of my friends, Paula and Jane, approached her and tried to begin a conversation with her. Tina was not terribly interested. Finally, Paula said, "Wouldn't you like to ask Jesus to come into your heart?"

Inwardly, I winced. Religious "jargon" always annoyed me and, besides, this girl was such an unlikely candidate for salvation that night.

If I had been upset by the abruptness of my friends' approach, I was even more upset by Tina's answer.

"I have no heart," she said.

Looking at her closely, I could almost believe it. Never had I seen such dead, listless eyes. Dull green, they held absolutely no expression.

"What do you mean you have no heart?" Jane asked quietly.

"I have no heart," the girl repeated.

"May we pray for you anyway? We'll ask Jesus to give you a heart," Paula said.

7

The girl shrugged.

Paula and Jane lightly placed their hands over the girl's head and began praying in English. After a few minutes they switched to their "tongue," the language each had received when she was baptized in the Holy Spirit.

Five minutes passed as I watched from a nearby seat. Surely, Jane and Paula had to realize they were wasting their time.

Ten minutes . . . I began to feel embarrassed for Tina. How was she going to escape my aggressive friends?

Fifteen minutes . . . Most people had left the church, and we were almost alone. I was physically uncomfortable and I wanted to go home.

Twenty minutes . . . At first, the sound was just a sigh. Then, softly, oh, so softly, Tina began to sob. Her crying became more intense. "Jesus," she cried. "I want You. Come into my heart."

In the seconds after she had sobbed those words, I saw something I have never seen before or after. I saw life come into those dead eyes that were now filled with tears and love. I literally saw her reborn.

In the combination of hugging, laughing, and crying that followed, I kept my eyes on Tina. She was a different person. This girl was animated; her face glowed. She was alive — really alive!

After a few more minutes, Tina was convinced she wanted the baptism of the Holy Spirit, too, and she received it along with her new heavenly language.

Since that day I have seen many miracles — legs lengthened, diseases halted, marriages restored, families reunited, but none of them compare with the miracle I saw that night when, despite my skepticism, I saw a girl actually "born again" through the power of the Holy Spirit.

What is the baptism of the Holy Spirit? It is the overflowing power of the Holy Spirit in the life of the believer. It is the conscious indwelling presence of that Comforter which Jesus promised He would send after He ascended to heaven, to lead us into "all truth" and enable us to do "even greater works" than He did.

In this book you will read the testimonies of women who have received the baptism of the Holy Spirit and are testifying to the changes the Holy Spirit has brought in their lives.

If you come from a denomination or a tradition that does not believe in the baptism of the Holy Spirit, I urge you to put aside your doubts for the time it takes you to read these testimonies. It could easily be one of the most valuable things you have ever done.

God bless you as you read.

Jo Anne Sekowsky

Is That All There Is To Life?

By Fran Lance

The matron came down the long hall, locking each door with keys clanging, and I heard the screams and hollers of the thirty other teen-age girls locked in with me. I looked through a barred window into the night sky, and in loneliness and desperation cried out to God my first prayer, "Is this all there is to life?"

Most of my sixteen years had been spent in foster and detention homes, and now I was in the Seattle Youth Center. A real home was unknown to me. My father had been killed on a motorcycle when I was four, leaving my mother with four small children. In her grief, she began drinking heavily, sometimes leaving us children for days at a time. Several times she unsuccessfully tried to take her life. Finally, the police came just in time to save her from one suicide attempt, and she was taken away on a stretcher. (I seldom saw her after that until years later when through a series of miracles I found her in Chicago.)

With no one to take care of me, I, along with the other children, became wards of the state of Washington.

"Although my father and my mother have forsaken me, yet the Lord will take me up [adopt me as His child]" (Ps. 27:10 TAB).

"Even as [in His love] He chose us — actually picked us out for Himself as His own — in Christ before the foundation of the world; that we should be holy (consecrated and set apart for Him) and blameless in His sight, even above reproach, before Him in love" (Eph. 1:4 TAB).

"You saw me before I was born and scheduled each day of my life before I began to breathe" (Ps. 139:16 TLB).

Yes, He has planned every day of my life, and He planned a warm Montana afternoon to touch my heart with His love. I was lying on my bed in a Great Falls detention home, full of self-pity and rebellion, when I heard a little girl singing, "It is no secret what God can do; what He has done for others He will do for you."

I remember wondering, "Well, what can God do for me?" because I had been searching for meaning in my life, trying to find satisfaction and comfort. What I really wanted was love and security, but the only road I knew was the wide road of self-satisfaction, pursuing my own fleshly desires. This was leading to my destruction, and even as a teen-ager I knew the road I was on would not satisfy.

I had been apprehended in Montana for delinquency, including drinking, running away and skipping school. Outwardly, I apppeared untouched by my confinement, for I had taught myself for years to hide my feelings. This was the only safe way to live. But inwardly, I was scared, lonely and desperately crying out for help. The adult world could only see the usual jubilant, confident, "nothing can touch me" Fran. No one knew the real Fran who longed to be loved.

No one knew but God! He knew, and He loved me as I lay on that bed with tears streaming down my cheeks.

The little girl singing was retarded and not even able to attend public school, but she sang God's message in a way that touched my rebellious heart.

The dinner bell rang and my "moment of weakness" was tucked way down inside until that lonely feeling came with the locking of the doors sometime later in the Seattle Youth Center.

As a ward of the state I was returned to Seattle when school was out in Montana and was placed in the Youth Center. When I cried out, "Is this all there is to life?" I know now that my heavenly Father answered me across the heavens that night and said, "No, there's much more!"

He didn't waste any time in directing my life toward those good things He had prepared because a few days later I was placed in the Washington Children's Home.

It was there that a Mr. Spencer called one evening to see if anyone wanted to attend the Billy Graham Crusade that was in

Seattle that summer of 1951. I responded to the invitation with the thought of leaving the meeting and getting downtown for some action with my cohorts, the same ones who had followed me into sneaking out at night, shoplifting and even stealing a car. But the Lord had other plans for that night!

He gave us no opportunity to sneak off. In fact, almost before we realized what was taking place, we were seated in the center of the Seattle Memorial Stadium with thousands of other people.

Billy Graham began telling us how we could start life all over, how our past would be completely forgiven, and that God would even forget the wrong things we had done.

"I, even I, am he that blotteth out thy transgressions for mine own sake and will not remember thy sins" (Isa. 43:25).

He said that our sins would be erased, completely removed, just as though we had never even committed them.

"As far as the east is from the west, so far hath he removed our transgressions from us" (Ps. 103:12).

I had never heard such good news! I was tired of my way of life; excitement wasn't enough any more. I wanted more from life but didn't know where to find it. Billy Graham was saying that Jesus is the answer, that I must invite Him to be the Lord of my life and accept Him as my Savior.

I wanted to change and hoped what Billy Graham was saying was true, because if Jesus couldn't save me from my old life, my old habit patterns, I knew there was no other way out.

We sang, "Just As I Am." What hope this song gave me! I had never heard it before; I had always thought you had to clean yourself up before coming to God. But the words said He accepted me just as I was. I stood there, sobbing and shaking. I wanted to go forward and accept Jesus, but the devil said, "If this doesn't work, your gang will make you a laughing stock."

Surely Billy Graham gave the longest altar call in history that night for me. Finally he said that none of us could know when our life might be taken and that we would go to hell if we had refused Jesus as our Savior. He said that somebody could get a knife in his back before he got home.

This was too real; I visualized it happening to me, and it was then that I stepped out, asking a friend to go with me. She did, and as we began the long walk down, I looked back. To my amazement the rest of the gang was following, including one of my own sisters. Hallelujah!

13

God drastically changed my life from that moment on. Now instead of using my flashlight to sneak out at night, I hid under the covers and used it to read a Bible story book from the school library. So great was my desire to know His Word, I even took notes on the stories. I had no other teacher. But the Holy Spirit was my teacher, just as Jesus said He would be. *". . . He shall teach you all things" (John 14:26). ". . . He will guide you into all truth" (John 16:13).*

For the first time I began to be aware of Jesus' love in other people, the Christians He brought into my life. These new friends trusted me in those early days when temptation was great. This meant so much because no one had ever trusted me before.

God not only changed my present life; He changed my plans for the future. Before I was saved I thought I would get an apartment with some girl, get a job and have lots of fun. I looked forward to not being under any authority, of being completely my own boss.

After Jesus came in, I didn't want to waste my life this way. Even though I had little confidence in my ability to go on in my education, somehow Jesus gave me the courage and a strong desire to go to college. As a ward of the state, I could have gone to a state college with all expenses paid, but I chose instead to go to a Christian college where I might learn more of my Lord and be with others who loved Him.

He opened the doors to get me started and then taught me to walk by faith for jobs. Each quarter I gained confidence as I was strengthened by Him. I often quoted, *"I can do all things through Christ which strengtheneth me" (Phil. 4:13),* and it became a reality in my life.

My senior year at Seattle Pacific College I married Russell Lance, a pre-seminary student. When my husband finished New York Biblical Seminary, we went as missionary-teachers to a mission in Sitka, Alaska.

My one desire was to do God's will and to bring others to Him. I poured my best efforts into the work of accomplishing this desire but saw few results. Something was missing, and the something was the direction and power of the Spirit for, *"it is the Spirit that quickeneth; the flesh profiteth nothing" (John 6:63).*

The students came to me, challenging the validity of the Scriptures, and I didn't know how to answer their questions. If I was going to continue in God's work, I had to have some answers.

We returned to Seattle after two years and adopted the first of our five children in 1963. As I held my tiny baby in my arms I knew I couldn't give him more of Jesus until I experienced more of Him myself.

This longing of my heart became a prayer which my heavenly Father was just waiting to hear. He sent a neighbor by who told me about the baptism in the Holy Spirit. The Lord knew my longing would cause me to listen with an open heart to a message I would have refused in the past. God's timing is always exactly right. *"As for God, his way is perfect" (Ps. 18:30).*

I heard Father Dennis Bennett, rector of St. Luke's Episcopal Church in Seattle, tell about the baptism in the Holy Spirit. He backed his testimony with Scripture and showed that Jesus the Baptizer is still baptizing believers today. *"For the promise is unto you, and to your children, and to all that are afar off, even as many as the Lord our God shall call" (Acts 2:39).*

I knew this experience was what I wanted, so with little emotion except for a little fear and self-consciousness, I asked Jesus to baptize me in the Holy Spirit.

I had asked to be filled with the Holy Spirit many times through the years and I know God did empower me, but it didn't seem to last. I had never spoken in tongues or been in fellowship with people who did, but in faith I yielded my pride to receive this blessing. I believed God would give me a language if I opened my mouth and began speaking. Feeling very foolish, yet wanting all God had for me, I became as a little child, and in seconds a language unknown to me began to flow.

How has this baptism of Jesus changed my life? First of all I must make it clear that my initial experience was just a doorway into a new reality of Jesus Christ. It has taken time to come on into the room, sit down, relax and sup with Him. I'm still eating the appetizers, and I know there are several courses yet to come. But I'm finding myself loving Him and expressing that love inwardly and outwardly unashamedly.

A new praise has welled up in my being and, as I allow this praise to be expressed, the joy of life comes forth and carries me above my problems and everyday circumstances. I know now that nothing can come into my life that my Father does not give His approval to. I know that He loves me so much that He is concerned even with the little details of the day and shares them with me.

My Comforter has taught me how to "yield" to Jesus' love instead of "trying" in my own efforts to achieve His will in my life. *"For it is God which worketh in you both to will and to do of his good pleasure" (Phil. 2:13).*

Jesus is everything to me. He has taught me that I am helpless without Him: *". . . for without me ye can do nothing" (John 15:5).*

He was and is the answer to the longing of my heart for love. He becomes more real each day as He reveals my need and teaches me how to yield to Him so that He might fill the need. I'm so glad I need Him!

Once I said, "Is this all there is to life?" Now I say, "Lord, give me a greater capacity to receive, for in You there is no limit!"

FRAN (Mrs. Russell) LANCE and her family attend Christ Church of Northgate in Seattle, Washington. They served two years on the Alaskan mission field under the Presbyterian Church. Russ is the athletic director and coach at King's Garden, an interdenominational Christian School. Fran formerly taught home economics there. They have five children: Dirk (9), Tami (8), Chad (6), Tracy (5) and Rusty (3).

Life's Deepening Glow Of Joy

By Genevieve Miller

Over fifty years ago, when I was a chubby, shy child, I thought: "If only Papa would go to church he would stop drinking; Mama would stop crying; and my sister, Doris, and I wouldn't have to be so afraid when we have to leave our friends each year to move to another little town."

For the sake of his wonderful old father, devoted wife and two little girls, all of whom he loved dearly, Papa wanted to stop drinking. He tried . . . and failed . . . and tried again, but his love for people and animals, physical strength and brilliant mind were not enough. It still saddens me to think how acceptance of God's help could have eased our family's burdens.

On each of Grandpa's annual visits he appealed to Papa's reason and his innate kindness. "Accept Jesus, son," he would beg. "Ask for forgiveness and strength from the Lord." But Papa's false pride boasted that he could stop the habit himself. And I truly believe that Papa did believe he could stop, so unfortunately, he substituted "will power" for "God power."

However, Papa did agree with Grandpa that my younger sister and I should become Christians, so in whatever shabby, rented house we lived, in whatever little town we moved to, Mama found the nearest church, no matter what denomination.

Lovingly, she brushed my sister's yellow curls around her finger and tied a ribbon around my brown hair. She dressed us in immaculate, dainty dresses she had made. Then, until we knew

17

the way, she escorted us to Sunday school and left us, confident that she was fulfilling her Christian duty. Occasionally Mama attended church, but the very special days were when Papa went, too, because his girls were taking part in the program.

I remember the Mother's Day program when I was eight. I surprised my parents by reciting this prayer which the Sunday school teacher had taught me:

> Lord Jesus, Thou hast known a mother's love and tender care,
>
> So for my own mother most dear I ask this birthday prayer:
> Protect her life, I pray, who gave the gift of life to me,
> And may she know from day to day
> Life's deepening glow of joy that comes from Thee.

After finishing, I took a deep breath and looked down into the congregation. Both Mama's blue eyes and Papa's big long-lashed grey ones were shining with tears.

Years later, I followed Mama's example. I sent my children to the nearest Sunday school but didn't go myself. "Why should I?" I asked myself. I was doing my Christian duty. I read my Bible, obeyed the Ten Commandments and committed only small sins, so what more could church do for me?

Eventually, I began attending the Episcopal church where, in time, I became confirmed and served on the Altar Guild committee. Our eldest daughter became a Sunday school teacher there and our son, an acolyte.

Perhaps to an outsider my life might have looked complete, but I knew it wasn't. I had many problems and the hardest to live with were the terrible fears that had begun in my childhood. Now that I was a grandmother my fears encompassed me so that my life was bound with fear. I'd been afraid when our eldest daughter nearly died from mastoid infection and when our son was ordered to Korea. Later I feared our grandson's heart surgery. I feared another grandson's epileptic seizures and feared for the future of our two teen-age granddaughters. I feared the bomb. And I was terribly afraid that the painful bursitis in my arms might become acute again.

This fear permeated my days until my second daughter, Marni, now a grown woman with two teen-agers, took me by the hand and led me to a different kind of life.

From her first Sunday school days, Marni had shown unmistakable signs of craving a deeper spiritual life. As she

18

became a curly-haired little rebel she started on her search: in the Lutheran, Episcopal, Salvation Army, and Independent Bible churches.

It still shames me to remember the day, when she was only seven, that Alma Enroth, a missionary in the Independent Bible Church, phoned us during services to say that Marni had requested to be baptized. Would we give our permission?

"Of course," I answered, my face burning as I climbed back up a ladder to the attic where my husband and I were pouring insulation between the rafters.

That same curly-haired little girl had never stopped her search for a meaningful life, one that would give her Jesus' help for raising her children and having a happier marriage, one that would make her His channel for helping others and one that would help her grow into physical, emotional and spiritual maturity.

She, too, "shopped around" for the denomination whose doctrine she could wholeheartedly accept. Then in Oregon, she found her answer, during a visit to a Portland church. The words of the evangelist there, the joyful expressions on the hundreds of young faces — many saved recently from drink and dope, and the exultation in the singing and shouts of praise made Marni want the "high" they were experiencing.

One day, at a full-gospel meeting in Portland, she received the warmth and overflowing joy of the baptism of the Holy Spirit. That night, alone on her knees in her bedroom, she received the gift of tongues. From then on Marni was a new woman. She felt a closeness to her husband; her love for everyone overflowed, and her face shone with joy as she placed her children under God's loving care.

Each time I visited her I saw more change. I attended church with her. I yearned more and more for the joy she possessed, but when she tried to tell me that God's gift was mine for the claiming, I lacked understanding.

"But I support my church," I qualified. "I help philanthropic organizations. I'm a director in the Humane Society and live by the Ten Commandments."

"But you are still afraid, Mom" she said gently.

I tried harder to get over my fears and to attain Marni's glow of joy. Finally she suggested my trouble. "Mom, you've been trying with your intellect, not your heart. You must have the faith of a child."

So I tried to have the faith of *my child;* I tried to forgive grievances, to discard resentment, to relinquish fear.

"When the devil tempts you with his tricks," Marni said, "picture Jesus quickly . . . His love . . . His compassion . . . His strength."

I did try.

Finally, at an evening youth meeting, the minister's message seemed somehow different. The sight of all those youths raising their arms in praise to God made the tears flood down my cheeks.

Marni whispered, "Mom, you feel the altar call, don't you?"

When I nodded she promised, "I'll go right behind you."

I walked down the aisle, unafraid of what others might think. As I knelt before the altar my tears were so noticeable that a sweet young girl came to pray for me. Marni knelt behind me, her arm on my right shoulder, her prayers mingling with mine.

But nothing dramatic happened. No warm surge, no heavenly light, no "high," no different tongues.

"Jesus," I prayed, "give me some sign. Just anything."

As Marni and I again sat in our seats she whispered, "Mom, accept your gift. Lift your arms in praise."

I did. And Jesus gave me my sign! My right arm, which had been filled with a mild but persistent pain of bursitis for fifteen years, shot up, easily, painlessly, joyfully. Marni's face lighted with happiness. "Praise the Lord, Mom!"

Thankfully, I echoed her praise.

Today, I praise the Lord every day, for each day I gain in compassion, understanding of His Word — and in peace about all that I once feared. I've since received my heavenly language. Now I'm experiencing what I asked for my dear mother over fifty years ago in that little Sunday school prayer, "Life's deepening glow of joy that comes from Thee."

GENEVIEVE (Mrs. Walter) MILLER and her husband live in Port Angeles, Washington, and are members of St. Andrew's Episcopal Church. Walter is a retired furniture store owner. Genevieve enjoys attending prayer groups and Women's Aglow Fellowships. She has been doing free-lance writing and has sold articles to Guidepost, Scripture Press and Free Methodist Sunday school papers. The Millers have four married children: Norman Miller, Ann Bender, Marni Gorski and Judy McBeath.

The Lord Is My Shepherd

By Claire Lasher

For the third time in a row the busy signal buzzed annoyingly in my ear and I banged the receiver back on the hook. Fuming, I thought of the inconvenience of not having my own phone and the frustrations of phoning in general in the Virgin Islands.

The incompleted phone call could have been a symbol of my life that day. Although I was a brand-new person in the Lord I had not yet received the joy and release promised to God's children. That was to come later. I waited for the phone to clear, questioning my sanity for ever having moved to the Caribbean.

I had moved from New Hampshire to the Virgin Islands in 1969 with Matthew, my seven-year-old son, to be near my parents, retired in St. Thomas. I acted sophisticated and charming, as if I hadn't a care in the world, but it was only a facade covering up the shattering effect of a heart-breaking divorce. At 104 pounds I was pitifully thin, smoking in spite of a history of TB and lung surgery, relying on sleeping pills and a drink or two to relax. Resentment and bitterness gnawed at me and an unreasonable temper simmered just below the boiling point.

But I was good at pretending I had my life under control, so with seven years' experience as a college French teacher, I was able to secure a job as teacher and assistant principal in a private school. Just as I appeared blase when I really wasn't, I also appeared religious and confident in my faith when actually I was nothing more than a restless, dissatisfied professing Christian. As

21

an intellectual, having studied toward a Ph.D., I acknowledged Jesus as the Son of God but never conceded Him as my Savior and my Lord.

The first year on the Island I put the lid on all my inner conflict, losing myself in my work, escaping in a constant round of social activities, cocktail parties and general "fun in the sun." I even contemplated remarriage.

In the process of climbing the professional ladder, I took a new job the following fall as an administrator of a small private school.

My landlady, Jo, doubled as my secretary. It's strange how well you can know a person and still not know her at all. I never dreamed that Jo was baptized in the Holy Spirit. Recognizing my deep hunger and longing, Jo gently led me to several Christian books, the most significant being Catherine Marshall's "Beyond Ourselves."

The reading of this book and others touched deeply into my spirit. I would lie in bed, after each day of pretense, and with every word read I would get a further glimmering of how phony my life was.

I became increasingly aware of the lack in my life of a real relationship with God in the person of Jesus Christ. It never occurred to me that Jesus meant it literally when He said, *"Behold, I stand at the door, and knock: if any man hear my voice, and open the door, I will come in to him, and will sup with him, and he with me" (Rev. 3:20).*

As I continued to read, the convicting power of the Holy Spirit took hold of me. Night after night I repented of all I could remember having done to grieve God and to separate myself from Him. I came to see that a formal church membership, a Christianity inherited from one's parents or an involvement in church activities was not the answer to entering the kingdom of God.

Finally came the night of September 28, 1970, when with a sigh of surrender I got down on my knees and said, "Lord, You are knocking, so I open my heart and ask You to come in."

Just as matter of factly I got up and went to bed, not realizing that I had taken a giant "leap of faith" and had at last accepted God's free gift. *"For by grace are ye saved through faith; and that not of yourselves; it is the gift of God; not of works, lest any man should boast" (Eph. 2:8-9).*

That night marked the beginning of a brand-new Claire Lasher. God had breathed His Spirit into my human spirit, forming a new creature with a change of direction. I began to pray, "Jesus, I am willing to do anything for You, go anywhere You want."

I suppose every new Christian hopes for instant peace. But that is not always God's way. Within one week, my job turned into a time of real tribulation. My faith was sorely put to the test, but I found myself strangely at peace in the midst of the crisis around me. At the end of three and a half months the situation was resolved — my duties were suspended, but my contract was honored, and I was granted six months' full pay.

This release from my job, which should have been an unnerving experience, left me free to read and to study. However, I had not yet learned to rest completely in the Lord, as my exasperation at the phone that day amply proved.

Drumming my fingers on the desk, I decided to try my phone call again — no luck. In a harried attempt to bide my time, I flipped open the fly-leaf of the nearest book which read, "Why would an established, well-respected Episcopal priest involve himself and his parishioners with the controversial 'speaking in tongues' experience?"

As an Episcopalian myself, I was literally horrified. "Speaking in tongues, an Episcopal priest? I can't believe it!" I rushed out onto the veranda, demanding to know where Jo had acquired this improbable story, *Nine O'Clock in the Morning,* by Dennis J. Bennett.

Jo was her usual serene self when I confronted her. "Why don't you read it yourself," she suggested, laughingly, "before you jump to conclusions?"

Frankly, I was not in the mood to read about this kind of nonsense, but I was free that day, so I reluctantly began reading the book.

Despite my preconceived ideas about Pentecost I found myself intrigued by Father Bennett's account of the great outpouring of the Holy Spirit today, accompanied by speaking in tongues, and of the way in which interdenominational prayer meetings were springing up all over the country as a result. There was only one such prayer group on St. Thomas, and it was in my neighborhood, one block away!

In the past I had carefully avoided accepting an invitation to these meetings, because I just knew they were wild, "holy roller" meetings. When I finally did go, out of curiosity more than anything else, what a surprise I had. The meeting was in the home of a college professor and his wife and there were some very normal people present — Lutherans, Methodists, Presbyterians, and even some Southern Baptists! Oh, the joy that shone from their faces and the love which they extended to me! I didn't even care that they were "fanatics."

I came home from that meeting realizing that these Spirit-baptized Christians had something I didn't have, and I wanted everything that God had to offer. If speaking in tongues was, in effect, the key which unlocked the door to the complete infilling and overflow of the Spirit, then I was willing to concede and turn that key.

Thus, in February, I went to the couple who headed the prayer group and asked them to pray for me. This they did gladly, but despite their prayers I felt nothing happen. I went home that night consoling myself with the idea that I was much too intelligent to speak something I didn't understand anyway.

In disappointment, I sat down to read the paper when it occurred to me that I *had* prayed in faith, believing. Deciding to thank God for having already received the baptism in the Holy Spirit I knelt to pray, noting that it was midnight. I opened my mouth to speak and from deep inside me came a welling-up of joy and then a stream of beautiful syllables which flowed forth with fluent ease.

I listened in wonder. Years of unexpressed joy surged forward, carrying in its wake pent-up fears, resentments, stresses and sorrows. The flood gates lifted and I began to cry tears of unhindered rejoicing. I had lifted my head and the King of Glory had come in! The Lord strong and mighty, the Lord mighty in battle had broken my chains and at last, I felt free! I felt clean. My soul was washed by the precious blood of Jesus and anointed in the Holy Spirit's "rivers of living water." I felt whole! As my tongue ceased proclaiming its freedom, I looked at the clock. I had been speaking in tongues for one hour and fifteen minutes.

For some time after that the words, "Living Springs Ranch" (a small Christian retreat center near Spokane, Washington) kept occurring to me. This retreat center had been mentioned in Father Bennett's book. When this happened again and again over a period of two weeks, I finally sat down and dashed off a brief job inquiry to Dean and Cordie Barber, the owners of the ranch.

The Holy Spirit prompted the Barbers to answer, encouraging me to join the ranch family as the Lord led. They had just been asking God to confirm the possibility of establishing a Christian satellite college when my letter arrived, inquiring if they could use the services of a teacher/administrator.

I was delighted at this "God's incident" but felt that I just had to have more confirmation. Being newly baptized in the Spirit, I had no idea that God has specific spiritual laws of guidance. In order to instruct me in His way, God led me to Miami to a Christian Growth Conference that May.

Midway through the conference, Bob Mumford gave an extensive teaching on guidance, now incorporated in his book, *Take Another Look at Guidance.* I took notes diligently as he delineated the three major ways in which God makes known and confirms His will. I understood what he called "the initial leading of the Holy Spirit" (His insistent prompting) from my own experience with this.

The second principle of guidance, that of the working together of circumstances of "Divine providence," I knew I had also experienced through my correspondence with the Ranch. Then he spoke of the third criterion, "confirmation in the written Word of God." I could in no way understand how I was going to open the Bible and see, "Go to Living Springs Ranch."

"I've had it!" I thought as I left the meeting, inasmuch as these three should line up in order for one to avoid being led astray.

The following day I was chatting idly with a friend when a plump little lady came up to us. I had never seen her before and noticed her "eyeing" me thoughtfully. She suddenly said to me, "The answer you are seeking you will find in Isaiah 58," and putting her hand on my head she continued, "and I am going to pray that God will make His will known to you in the reading of His Word." My heart seemed to be running away with itself and I felt a warmth envelop me. She was a Spirit-baptized minister from California who said God had sent her to this conference to deliver messages to two people. I was the second. With her mission accomplished, off she went!

Rather stunned, I sought an opportunity to be thoughtfully alone with God's Word. As I read Isaiah 58, my heart began to race again and when I came to verse eleven the words seemed to jump out at me six inches high on the page, *"And thou shalt be like a watered garden, and like a spring of water, whose waters fail not."* I remembered a verse of Scripture at the top of the Living Springs Ranch brochure. I grabbed my Ranch correspondence from my suitcase in such haste that the brochure spiraled to the floor. There it was, staring up at me again — Isaiah 58, verse 11!

I wondered if this was what Bob Mumford meant by confirmation in the Word of God. Sometime later, while sharing with Bob this beautiful example of the principles which God had shown him, I told him my story. He listened pensively. When I had finished, he said slowly, "I feel that God may have a reason quite different than what you think for taking you to Washington, and that you should remain flexible and open to whatever He has planned for you, whether this college develops or not."

At these words of knowledge and wisdom, peace flooded me and I remembered that shortly before my baptism in the Spirit I had yielded to God all rights to myself and to my life, willing to do anything for Him and to go anywhere He wanted me to go, and now He was taking me up on my offer. Within a month, my son and I were on our way to Washington, 5,000 miles away!

Three years have passed since that day I reluctantly began reading *Nine O'Clock in the Morning*. And here at the Ranch, I still marvel at all that has happened since that day. God indeed has had a different plan for me than I had envisioned. The college, as such, has not evolved, but Living Springs Ranch has been my place of nurture while God has had me in His school of the Holy Spirit. While training me, God has been bringing my life into His divine order, and has established a "head" for me in the mature eldership of this small retreat center.

Through the scriptural use of the rod, in love, further establishing Christ as the head of our household of two, Matthew is learning God's divine order in his young life as well. Shortly after my transforming baptism in the Spirit, he received Jesus as his Savior. Six weeks after arriving at Living Springs Ranch, Matthew spoke in tongues spontaneously one night while saying his bedtime prayers.

Jesus the Healer has touched me in body as well as soul and spirit, healing my lungs, my eyes and a capricious slipped disc.

But the most glorious healing of all has been the emotional restoration which the Great Physician has wrought in my life. The Holy Spirit has dealt with my soul (my emotions, my mind, and my will) bringing repentance for my sins, my forgiveness of the people who have hurt me, and deliverance as I have loosed unto God the Father all the resentments I had stored away. I no longer need to smoke or drink or take sleeping pills, and my temper has come under control as Jesus continues His healing processes in my soul. No longer do I pretend I'm something that I'm not.

Supplying *all* my needs, God has allowed me to travel with Matt thousands of miles to witness and minister about the baptism in the Holy Spirit, including a trip to Germany.

Truly I can say with the psalmist, *"The Lord is my shepherd . . . He refreshes and restores my life — my self" (Ps. 23:1,3 TAB)*.

CLAIRE LASHER now lives in Spokane, Washington, where she regularly teaches several Bible studies in addition to conducting a weekly fellowship for single women. She is worship chairman of the Spokane Women's Aglow Fellowship and has been a speaker for the Tri-Cities WAF as well as many others. Claire has a B.A. from Keuka College and an M.A. from Middlebury College French School. She studied in Cardiff, Wales, and worked briefly in Paris before pursuing studies toward a Ph.D. in French literature at the universities of Massachusetts and New Hampshire prior to becoming a school administrator in the Virgin Islands. Her busy schedule includes editing for World Missionary Assistance Plan and acting as treasurer for the Northwest Christian Fellowship of Spokane. She and her son, Matthew, attend the Church of the Rock of Ages.

Faith, Not Feeling

By Pat King

There were four of us in the tiny parlor of St. Mary's convent, the three sisters who taught my children and me. The prayer of the nuns was simple, "Come, Lord Jesus, hear the prayer of Your child, Pat, and fill her with Your Holy Spirit."

No wind whistled through the room. No tongues of flame hovered visibly. Except for the prayer of four women, all was still. Yet, there in the quiet, the Holy Spirit came upon me and a new but old language came to my tongue. New because I was consciously aware of it. Old because I recognized it as words I had somehow prayed before. That was all.

No, there was none of the exhuberant joy, no releasing tears, none of the many marvelous signs of the Holy Spirit that other people raved about. Oh, well, maybe tomorrow it would come. It didn't though, not the next day or the next day or the next. I knew I had been baptized in the Holy Spirit, but I didn't feel a thing.

I had heard people say that their new language was so comforting they could hardly stop praying in it. I prayed in mine but it was like praying the divine office (a liturgical prayer of the Catholic church). It was warm and familiar but just not exciting.

Others said that after they had been baptized in the Holy Spirit the Bible became so compelling they couldn't put it down. I opened up my Bible, ready for this experience, but the words didn't leap out and mesmerize me with new understanding. They were the same words I had heard at Bible camp as a child and

29

read in the morning at Mass as an adult.

Perplexed, I wrote a letter to an old friend, the man who wrote *They Speak In Other Tongues*. Certainly John Sherill would be able to help me.

He answered: "My dear Pat, the main thing I want to say is that your baptism is typical of many Roman Catholics. It has been my experience that some Romans receive a quite different type of experience . . . it is in keeping that no lights flashed for you . . . "

It was nice of John to answer, but he offered little comfort.

I was still mulling over my situation several days later when my fifth child, Johnny, came down to breakfast. Johnny is generally unhappy in the morning and his crabbiness inevitably makes me crabby too. That morning Johnny greeted the day by snapping that there was a lump in his oatmeal and he wasn't going to eat the dumb old stuff. Ordinarily I would have snapped right back at him.

That morning I took the lump out and kissed him on the cheek. Without another complaint he picked up his spoon and finished his cereal.

Hmmmm, that was odd. Many times before I'd known I should answer him kindly, but I had never been able to get past feeling irritated.

Just a couple of days later over pizza in a little Italian restaurant, my husband tried to talk to me about his negative feelings toward the whole charismatic movement. My temper flared and while the pizza grew cold our conversation grew icy. The evening would have been a complete disaster except that I excused myself and went to the ladies' room. There in the dimness I prayed in the tongue given me. It was still unexciting but, when I stopped, the resentment and anger in me was gone. The rest of the evening I listened to his objections and loved him for being honest with me.

The following week a neighbor sat down at the kitchen table and burst into tears. There was so much agony in her life she couldn't face it any longer.

For some reason I put my hand over her clenched fist and said, "Let's pray about it." The words of prayer came easily to my lips. I couldn't believe I'd had the courage to pray out loud in front of someone.

My neighbor dried her eyes and smiled. "Thank you, I feel a

lot better now. A strange thing happened to me when you began to pray. I felt a warmth go through my body and somehow comfort me."

"Oh, no," I thought to myself, "I didn't feel a thing."

After that there were too many personal victories to ignore. I was more patient with all my children. I did win battles with my temper and resentment. I was able to pray with people who needed help. The Bible was still the same familiar words, but I found my Bible reading time pre-empted far less by other cares.

There wasn't a victory every time but they were growing enough to tell me there was a power in my life that was helping me each day.

So now I have quit looking for the "religious experience," knowing that the Holy Spirit is mine and He will help me no matter what I feel inside.

PAT (Mrs. William) KING is a free-lance writer, associate editor of Aglow Publications when she isn't busy being a mother to her ten children. A Catholic, Pat now lives in Kent, Washington. Her husband, Bill, works for the Boeing Company and is Aglow Publications' financial advisor. Pat has authored three books for Logos and has recently compiled an Aglow book entitled HEALED.

Daddy Never Said, "I Love You!"

By Jerry Witt

In early 1971 my husband, Troy, and I were looking forward to a four-week vacation. For the first time in our married life we had the time and money to make the trip possible. In early April we received a letter from a friend of my father, saying Daddy had a growth in his lungs and faced major surgery. She mentioned the dread word — "cancer."

No matter how much I hated the idea, I knew I would have to postpone the vacation and go to my father. I was the oldest of four children, the only daughter. My father had drunk from the time I could remember. My memories were of coming home with a drunken father driving, swerving from one side of an Oklahoma country road to the other. My parents had never shown any affection to each other and, even as a tiny girl, I had sensed their unhappiness. I was never held in my father's lap or told I was loved. How I yearned to be loved by him. I always felt he loved my brothers more than me, if indeed, he loved me at all!

When I was thirteen, my mother left Daddy to go live with another man whom she later married after her divorce became final. Now, I was pulled in two directions. One part of me yearned for my mother while my heart broke for my father. He began to drink heavily and it humiliated me terribly. I quit school because I could no longer concentrate and I went back and forth from one parent to the other. So, I grew up feeling unloved and unwanted. Hostility after hostility grew in my heart toward

33

Daddy, as well as toward many others. Even in later years when Daddy did come to visit us I bitterly resented him, for he would always be drinking. Our sons noticed and told me I was mean to my own daddy.

Now, word came that Daddy had cancer; I went to him, not from love, but because he was old, alone, and it was my duty. We were there a day or so before he went in for surgery. My brother and his wife from Arizona came to be with us. Here Daddy was facing major surgery, and we all knew, including him, that he might not live through the surgery. He wasn't drinking now; he was sober and reaching out. God forgive me — I could not show him any love!

It was Troy and my brother who asked him about his relationship to Jesus. "I know Jesus as my Savior," he assured us. "I accepted Him when I was young." He looked at us around his bed and tears filled his eyes. "I was always so proud that my kids knew Jesus, too."

He was in surgery many hours; then the doctor finally came out and told us he was in recovery, but they were not able to remove all the cancer cells. He suggested radiation therapy and said Daddy probably would not live over a year. We talked it over and decided to move him close to us in Vista, after he recuperated sufficiently. Daddy had no choice but to agree, for he would need help in the future.

After we got home, I began to realize what a tremendous job I had ahead of me. I resented it and did not want to be burdened with a father who drank and whom I did not love.

I gave up all my duties at the church because I knew taking care of him would take all my time. I especially resented giving up my job as youth director, and I cried, feeling cheated and bitter.

In five or six weeks my brother and his wife brought Daddy to live in a quiet trailer park near town. We were amazed at how well he made the trip, but he was very thin and weak.

I was also amazed at how the Lord was giving me wisdom and strength to do the things regarding Daddy that had to be done. We began his radiation therapy. I'd take him to the hospital each morning and when I would return in the afternoon, he would be so drunk that he could not talk sensibly. As I look back, I realize he was lonely and afraid of facing pain and eventual death. I hated his drinking, but found myself, on several occasions taking him to the store to buy wine. Even while I began to grow closer to

34

Daddy I kept backing off, hanging onto my hostilities.

Something was wrong in my life. I began to realize that, as a Christian, I was somehow missing the mark. Where was the joy, peace and assurance that Christians were supposed to have? Thus began my search — a battle between Satan and God — that lasted for months.

I began talking to my doctor, who was also Daddy's doctor. I explained my tensions and hostilities to him. He told me not to worry, that I had done everything a daughter could do, but in my heart I knew that wasn't enough. Oh, how I wanted to love my daddy and be loved in return! Finally in near desperation, I went to our pastor with my problems. He told me that there were hostilities in my life, and until I rid myself of them, I could never be the effective Christian God wanted me to be. He prayed with me, and I left, feeling just as burdened as when I had entered his office. I knew he was right, but I hadn't learned where to leave those hostilities.

We were getting ready for a revival in our church. Our pastor had sent mimeographed sheets with prayer requests and Scripture for each day into every home. I began to read these, praying each day that the Lord would remove my hostilities and give me a clean heart.

Nothing had changed with Daddy. I'd go to see him, and in five minutes I'd get so disgusted because he would be drunk that I would storm out. I'd go only a few blocks before I'd ask God's forgiveness for being critical. I'd feel so ashamed that I could not love my father as he was. However, this pattern continued.

Then on the fifth day, after I had been reading God's Word and praying for a clean heart, cleansing tears began flowing down my cheeks, saturating the front of my blouse. I was totally immersed in God's love from head to toe. Wave after wave of His cleansing love filled my being, and I began to laugh and praise the Lord. And when it was over — praise the Lord — all my hostilities were gone. I felt such peace and love within myself, and how I loved Jesus. That day I felt I could never love Him more, but He becomes more precious each day. Oh, the joy of being freed from hostilities, to be able to love freely and reach out for love. The joy of being able to say, "Praise the Lord," and mean it with all my heart!

From that time on, my obligation to Daddy became a joy. I was filled with a peace I'd never dreamed possible. I began to see everything in a different light. I began to search the Scriptures and set aside a time each morning to talk to God. I'd been so critical toward so many in my life, and the Holy Spirit began to convince me to go to them and ask their forgiveness. If it wasn't possible to talk to them, I called or wrote a letter and explained what had happened to me. People began to tell me there was a change in me. Songs had new meaning; songs I'd sung for years became so meaningful and the words so precious, and so did the Bible, God's wonderful book that I'd neglected so many years. Now there is peace, joy and power in life. Each new day is so exciting, for it is God's day for me.

On December 19th, Daddy's condition worsened, and we admitted him to a convalescent center. As he grew weaker he reached out more and more to the Lord. I grew to love him so much and yet I prayed that he be spared the horrible pain that terminal cancer brings. God honored that request. About twenty hours before the Lord took him, Daddy rallied from a coma, reached out and took my hand. For the first time he said the very words I had yearned to hear all my life, "Jerry, honey, I love you."

"Daddy, I love you, too!"

These were the last words we said to each other.

It was a gift from God that I will always treasure, but a gift He could only give after He had taken away the hostilities in my heart.

JERRY (Mrs. Troy) WITT and her husband live in Vista, California, and are members of Vista Christian Center. They have a married son, Don (26), and another son, Gary (23). Troy is a supervisor for Golden Arrow Dairy and is presently chairman of the Board of Trustees of their church. Jerry has a telephone ministry and loves to write and sing in the choir.

Miracles—
By The Power
Of His Spirit

By Shura Temoschenko

In 1932 a group of Russian Christians began making their way into China because of a great famine and starvation that had been predicted by the Holy Spirit in several meetings. My parents were members of this group. After a journey of about two years, they found their way into Kuldja, a city about fifty miles from the border of the Soviet Union in mainland China.

The crossing of the border was indeed miraculous. The guards were sleeping, and not one of them even heard the noise of footsteps, of pots and pans, and of babies crying just a few feet away from them. And so, a new life, a new country, a new language awaited my family, with all its problems of political and economical unrest.

In the very beginning, life in mainland China, as I knew it, was good and provided for us all that was needed. I was born there, I grew and got acquainted with the customs and ways of living of that great and very crowded country. Since many of our Christian friends had found refuge in our area we had a good-sized congregation on Sundays, and our Christian life and fellowship was very active, without any obstacles from the authorities for fifteen years.

In 1949, the atheistic powers took over in China. Then we discovered the full meaning of a life of struggles, persecutions and harassments. It was so bad that we could not profess our faith in the living God openly. We turned to the Holy Spirit for guidance,

37

strength, and comfort. Often, during times of prayer and worship, He would speak to us. In His wonderful omniscience He would reveal to us ahead of time the freedom and prosperity of a land that was unknown to us, and often referred to as a place of paradise here on this planet of ours. It was a land where we could worship our God in full freedom, read His Word and sing to Him at any time and anywhere, without being constantly subjected to repression.

It took about fifteen years of prayers and expectancy before we saw the fulfillment of this prophetic promise of God. One day, in the middle of a Sunday worship service, a representative from the government came and announced clearly and briefly some words that I will hear echoing in my ears until Jesus comes: "You are free to leave China any time!"

After a journey of several thousand miles on uncovered government trucks, and after being rained and snowed upon a number of times, we arrived in Hong Kong. From there we went to the land God had promised to us: Sydney, Australia.

The Lord saved me and baptized me in His wonderful Holy Spirit while we were still in China. Our faith and His love and guidance are what kept all of us trusting and hoping that somewhere beyond the horizon was a better future. I was the second child in a family of fifteen children and felt responsible for the upbringing and care of the rest of the family since mother's health was not always the best. They all live in Adelaide, Australia, now and all of them belong to Jesus.

About seven years ago, I felt prompted by the Lord to come and visit the United States. I came on a 28-day excursion trip with my Uncle Paul to visit some of our Russian Christians in San Francisco. I stayed on and the Lord opened up to me a wonderful ministry in teaching the Russian language and taking part in some of the radio ministries to our people behind the Iron Curtain. The Lord gifted me in writing poems in Russian and often inspires me to write for His glory. This may be a very small ministry, but I have made it a point in my life to use my freedom in any way possible so that the wonderful message of God's love and the sacrifice of His Son will be known to our people wherever they are.

In January, 1970, our church in San Francisco was visited by a young evangelist of Russian heritage from Europe who held a series of meetings throughout the Bay area. After a few days in our church he asked if he could speak to me privately. As we had lunch together he boldly confessed to me that the Lord had revealed to him that I would be his companion and asked me to pray about this matter. I was amazed and confused, and I did not know what to say. But I really started to pray from that day on and sought God's guidance. After several days the answer came clearly and plainly. A few weeks later we were married at the Russian Gospel Temple in San Francisco.

I continue to marvel as I see how God guides us and cares for us, especially now that Tony and I are engaged in a full-time work among our people and wherever the Lord leads us.

Some have said that I should forget my past experiences in China, all the misery, starvation, and poverty. But on the contrary, I think about all that quite often. It makes me more thankful to God for what I see and am able to have here in this wonderful country. Sometimes I feel so sad when I see the young American generation so unappreciative and so unsatisfied, some rebelling, some constantly complaining, some leading a life without purpose in drugs.

My heart cries out for the women who have unsaved children or husbands. But if God made such a great miracle for us in China, I know He can do the same here in America. God's Word indicates that Jesus was not able to perform miracles in some places because "they believed Him not." I know that when we start really believing, our Lord does the rest, the answering.

Some time ago He answered prayers for us and for another group of Russian believers in China, that the Chinese government had released after 22 years of praying and believing. This group of God's children is in Hong Kong right now and should be in Australia soon. Some of them are distant relatives to me and my parents. We hope to see them soon as we plan to be in Australia ourselves in a few days.

My parents live in Australia, along with my eight brothers and five sisters. God has really done wonderful things in our family. There were days when we did not have anything for the morning breakfast, but always, in some strange and mysterious way, the Lord would speak to somebody in Australia or America and we would receive $10, or sometimes even $20, which helped us to feed the whole family for almost a month.

Living in America makes the past sometimes seem like a dream, and often I really must make an effort to realize that this is the life for which we had been praying for a number of years with only the hope that some day our wishes would become a reality. But I sincerely believe that the Lord did not bring us to this wonderful land just to sit down and enjoy it. God knew that here in the free world we could do much more for His kingdom, and this is the prime reason why I believe He helped us to come here. He has given us a burden for our people in Russia, China, Australia, here and wherever they are.

Here at the San Francisco Russian Gospel Temple, we are able to reach all those people in their various lands through the radio ministry which operates through stations as far away as Portugal, the North Pole, and the Philippines. These programs broadcast the full-gospel of Jesus Christ on a daily schedule. We also have some radio ministries throughout the United States, in areas densely populated by our people.

If you ever happen to be in San Francisco, let me invite you to come and visit us on Sunday and hear the beautiful Russian Gospel Choir at 2233 - 17th Street and meet people like Brother Shevchenko, the pastor, or my Uncle Paul Ionko, who heads the radio department. Just about all the members of the Russian Gospel Temple are from Russia or are Russian young people born in China.

As we leave for a visit to Australia we hear reports of the Lord doing some great things. There were some Australian Roman Catholic nuns who came to a Russian meeting and, while they did not understand a word, were filled with the Holy Spirit. Four of my brothers have received the baptism in the Spirit just recently there. We expect much greater things to happen because we sincerely believe that we are living in the time prophesied in Joel 2:28 right now, for it was said that in the last days, *"I will pour out my spirit upon all flesh."*

SHURA (Mrs. Tony) TEMOSCHENKO and her husband are in full-time Christian ministry. Of Russian heritage, Shura was born in China, lived in Australia and now resides in Woodburn, Oregon. Shura and Tony have a radio ministry. They also travel as a team to evangelize and testify about Jesus Christ and have recently returned from Russia. They are members of the San Francisco Russian Gospel Temple.

Frosting On The Cake

By Ethel Jones

It happened of all places, in a large gathering of Christian women busily drinking coffee and discussing plans for a Bible study retreat. I had managed to finagle myself across the room so that I could sit beside a gal I admired very much, one of those fun people who glows and makes you feel good to be with. Later, I was to discover she had literally prayed me across the room.

All I can remember about the conversation is asking her how come she, with three little kids, could look so happy and peaceful while I, with only two, could feel and look like the wreck of the Hesperus. Grinning, she lowered her voice and said, "It's because I have the frosting on the cake."

Now, perhaps some people could have passed that off but not me. Four years of journalism training in "who, what, where, when and why" caused me to investigate. About a million questions later I walked out of the meeting with mixed emotions and a paper bag containing a copy of Larry Christenson's *Speaking in Tongues*.

I kept telling myself all the way home, "I don't need it . . . it reeks with emotionalism." Those in the Bible class I was teaching considered it paganistic. I felt the only thing to do was to give the bag back, unopened.

Many hours later, dinner still unstarted, I was avidly re-reading chapter 5: "Is Speaking in Tongues for Me?" I slammed the book closed, stuffed it back in the bag and said very

41

definitely, "No!" I had been born again fourteen years ago, I had received the Holy Spirit, and that was all I needed!

Next, I was plagued with a conspiracy of well-meaning friends who said I simply had to go to St. Luke's Episcopal Church and hear Father Dennis Bennett's story. I went voluntarily and listened with a journalistic ear. It was a great story . . . and I thought . . . "bully for him." He needed it; I didn't.

Then why, I would ask myself as I crossed the Lake Washington floating bridge and headed for St. Luke's for the umpteenth time, why do you keep going back? Well, I reasoned, it feels good just being there. What? I thought. Now you're going on feeling. You know how you feel about people who go on feelings. So, around and around I went. I was becoming impossible to live with, and finally even my long-suffering gentle dog would see me coming and run for parts unknown.

On my weekly pilgrimages to St. Luke's I'd buy dozens of books which I'd all but inhale. Then, I'd proceed to annoy all my "frosting friends" with questions, more questions, and even repetitions of the first questions. The miracle is that they loved me through it all.

Now, I might have gone on like this forever, but a very strange thing happened to me at the Bible study retreat. A dear Christian lady spoke on, "Why I don't think it's necessary in this age to speak in tongues." All of a sudden deep down inside me something felt wounded, deeply hurt, and I didn't quite know why.

That summer was spent practically in isolation seeking God in a new, agonizing way. Oh, the questions I threw at Him, the longings that brought pools of tears to the surface. I felt lost. Our modern liberal church services had no meaning, no depth for me and I would leave unfilled, unhappy and oh, so hungry for a deeper walk with God.

We all have a saturation point. One September afternoon, after lunching with a dearly beloved Spirit-filled friend, we sat and talked in her car in the parking lot. It was a special day, my husband's 45th birthday, and I had to hurry home and bake his favorite cake. I can remember how very hurt I was because my friend had also reached her saturation point with me. She was telling it like it was and I didn't want to hear it.

"You're trying too hard to analyze God. You're too intellectual, Ethel. God can't be dissected."

I managed to give her a smile, got into my car and began driving home, yelling at God all the way. "All right, God, I give up. I don't care if I ever speak in tongues. All I want to do is Your will. I love You and that's all that matters."

Zap! I felt different, released, happy, and I sang the rest of the way home. I was still singing as I beat the cake batter. My seventeen-year-old daughter, Maureen, was curled up on the sofa, studying her lines for the school play. Suddenly she appeared in the doorway. "Mom, you didn't take Russian in college, did you?"

"What are you talking about? Of course, I didn't take Russian."

"Well, you're singing Russian or something Slavic."

"I am? How do you know?"

"Well, we've been listening to tapes of Russian to get our accents right for the play, and you sound like the tape. Hey, is that the speaking in tongues bit?"

I opened my mouth and experimented. Words of a completely foreign flavor came out. "Well, I guess that's what it is all right," I said.

No flashing lights, no tears, no nothing, but new strange-sounding words. I called my beloved friend and stated, "It happened and I don't feel different at all."

Exactly two weeks later I knew why I had had such a desperate desire for this baptism in the Holy Spirit. I was told that my wonderful, beloved husband had acute leukemia. There were not enough words to help me cry out to God in my anguish. As I knelt by our bed, suddenly a flow of new words came forth and soared up to God. Suddenly I felt released and surprisingly peaceful. I was surrounded and protected by a warm feeling of God's love. I knew that He was forever with me in a special way.

Frosting? Well, hardly. Rather, one of the main ingredients giving body, texture and a very special flavor to the cake. Everyone, but everyone, should have such frosting.

ETHEL (Mrs. Floyd) JONES is the mother of two children, a married daughter, Maureen, and a son, Mike, who attends Christ For the Nations' Bible Institute in Dallas, Texas. Ethel majored in journalism at Wayne State University in Detroit, Michigan. Her husband was an aeronautical engineer at the Boeing Company for 17 years. Now a resident of Bellevue, Washington, Ethel attends the Neighborhood Assembly of God.

Ours For The Asking

By Betty Denham

I think most Christian growth is a slow process—a gradual unfolding of our awareness of God and the deeper things of life. Just as a mighty oak tree grows slowly as it sinks its roots deep into the earth, so our souls expand slowly as we nourish them with spiritual food. I was never really conscious that I did not know how to pray until there was a great need in my life to contact God. Then I realized just how shallow my prayer life had been. A small intercessory prayer group taught me the meaning of prayer. But learning to abide in the presence of God seemed only to make me more conscious to other needs—the most urgent one being that, while I had accepted Jesus as my Savior, I had never really experienced anything that made God vitally real to me. I had simply grown up in the Methodist church, joined at the age of nine and had not grown in knowledge of the Lord at all. I had been teaching Sunday school since I was eighteen, been active in the WSCS and now the Guild, been in choir for years and had served in almost every capacity as an officer in the church. I was doing the "works" but it is not enough just to work for the Lord. Without a vital encounter with Him, my works were in vain! Oh, I had had several mountain-top experiences, and they were simply wonderful, but they did not last. As soon as the glow faded I was right back in the same ol' rut doing the same ol' things time after time.

Every now and then I would see in the paper where some

church was to have a speaker to talk on the subject of the Holy Spirit. This was something I had never quite understood. I would always prick up my ears and did manage to attend a few of these meetings. But it seemed to me the speakers talked in circles and left me more confused when it was over than when it began.

Then one day it happened! I was talking to one of the local Episcopal clergy, Father Hall, and he told me an Episcopal priest, Father Dennis Bennett, was coming from Seattle to speak on the Holy Spirit. He also said there was a tape recording available of a talk Father Bennett had made in Miami. I asked if we might borrow the tape to have a "sneak preview" in our prayer group before Father Bennett came.

We played it that Thursday night and were impressed. On Saturday afternoon, about four o'clock, one of the prayer group members called to tell me there would be an informal meeting at a private home that night at which Father Bennett would speak. She suggested that I go and represent the prayer group and bring back to them as much "inside information" as possible.

I did not see how I could go. I had just washed my hair. I had supper to prepare for six people. It was just impossible! Well, she insisted, so I called the number she gave me and spoke to Darrel Hon, who, at that time was a complete stranger to me. I asked if I might come to the meeting.

He was cautious over the phone (I am sure he felt I was merely a curiosity seeker) and said that this was not just "a meeting." There were to be a few people coming for the baptism of the Holy Spirit. A few others were coming to pray with them that they might receive this baptism. I said I would like to come and pray with them.

Then he asked me point-blank if I wanted to be baptized in the Holy Spirit. Well, I did not know what he was talking about and was so taken aback that I started stammering and stuttering, "Oh, no, I don't want to receive the Holy Spirit. I just wanted to meet Father Bennett informally. I plan to hear him speak tomorrow night, and the prayer group thought it would be nice for me to meet him and tell them all about it." Mr. Hon said I could come, but I could tell he had reservations, and so did I.

When I arrived at the Hon's they were both so cordial and gracious to me that I immediately felt at home. I did not know it at that time, but their home is so filled with the presence of the Holy Spirit that you can feel it as soon as you go in.

About twenty-five people were there, and when Father Bennett came in he sat down and immediately started a period of instruction. When he finished he asked to see the hands of those who had come to receive the baptism in the Holy Spirit. My hand went up of its own volition. I did not consciously raise it! I looked at my hand and was horrified. I thought to myself, "I did not come here for this and here I am with my hand raised." I didn't know what to do. I thought it would be embarrassing to lower my hand after having raised it.

Father Bennett said he would take us two at a time (there were six who raised their hands) and we were to go into the next room. He asked that only a few persons, who felt definitely led of the Lord, to come in and pray with us. The rest were asked to remain where they were and pray. Six came in to pray. The lady who went in with me was Josie Wright, a Catholic.

Josie and I were seated in chairs and the others stood around us to pray. Father Bennett laid his hands on her head and prayed that she would receive the baptism in the Holy Spirit. In a few moments Josie began speaking in an unknown tongue. It was undoubtedly the most beautiful sound I have ever heard. It was like an ancient chant, so melodious, half singing—half speaking, just indescribably beautiful. I was fascinated! They prayed for her a few minutes longer, praising God and thanking Him for this glorious manifestation of His Spirit.

Then Father Bennett came over to me and laid his hands on my head and prayed. For a moment nothing happened. Then a wonderful sense of peace came over me and I knew all was well. After the peace came the joy. Oh, the joy of Jesus is so wonderful!

Father Bennett instructed me to start praying in English and assured me that an unknown tongue, the language of the Spirit, would follow. All I could say was, "Thank You, Father," which I repeated several times. And then my little "word" came. It was not beautiful and melodious like the words in Josie's language; in fact, it sounded quite silly. This was more like stammering lips than anything else. (Since that time I have a language all my own, and it is so wonderful to be able to pray in the Spirit and know that whatever I am saying is exactly what He wants to hear!)

I began to laugh, whereas Josie was crying. I had never felt such joy and peace. After a few minutes of repeating my little "word" Father Bennett asked me to interpret. My mind went absolutely blank. I had no earthly idea what I had been saying. So

I just waited, not knowing what to say. Then these words came, "Thus saith the Lord, 'I will strengthen you for the tasks that lie ahead. I will go with you all the way, yea, even unto the end.'"

He has strengthened me, for I have received power to be a witness for Him and power to live an overcoming life when temptations surround me. Now don't misunderstand me; I am far from being perfect, but it is so wonderful to know that when we are faced with problems we can take them to Him, and He has the answer! And even when we fail and stumble and fall, He is there to raise us up and to guide us back into His paths and into His ways.

I laughed all the way home, drunk on the "new wine." The joy of the Spirit is so wonderful! When you have this experience you truly are a new creature. Everything is different! The grass is greener; the sky is bluer; the birds sing more sweetly and best of all, you are aware of the needs of others around you. The compassion of Jesus is born in you and you yearn to help others and to tell them of the glorious relationship with Jesus the Christ while we are still here on this earth.

There has been so much said recently about the baptism in the Holy Spirit, and especially the speaking in a heavenly language, that many people are confused and even averse to the idea because they feel it is too emotional. Well, praise God, for me it was an emotional experience. After all, God is love and love is certainly the greatest of all emotions.

We need instruction in the meaning of the baptism in the Holy Spirit. Today the church is impotent in many areas of Christianity. She has lost her original power because her people do not have this power as individuals to go about doing the Father's business, witnessing for Him and overcoming temptations in their daily lives and praying for the sick to be healed. This was the secret of the strength of the early Church and the early Christians. Each new convert was instructed to receive the baptism in the Holy Spirit.

When Paul visited the church in Ephesus someone must have neglected to do this, for the first thing he asked was, *"Did you receive the Holy Spirit since you believed?" (Acts 19:2).* He could tell immediately something was lacking. Where was the joy, the fire? Where was the glow on the faces and the light in the eyes of these disciples? If you walk in the Spirit there is a glow.

We, as Christians, need to be asked this question today,

"Have you received the Holy Spirit since you believed?" If you answer with the Ephesians, "We don't know what you are talking about," then as you read the rest of this witness, I pray that the Spirit Himself will quicken you and open your heart to an understanding of this wonderful manifestation. It's up to you to accept it or reject it, but at least you will know about it!

The Bible says that when the Spirit has come, we will speak with other tongues and magnify God, as the Spirit gives us utterance. This is the scriptural sign of the baptism in the Holy Spirit. There need be no excessive emotional display, although this could happen. Many people do receive the baptism without emotion. All you have to do to receive Him is to surrender completely and ask Him to baptize you with the Holy Spirit and He will do it. Someone has said it is not so much what we will do with the Holy Spirit in our lives, but what we will allow Him to do with us that counts in the long run.

BETTY (Mrs. Don) DENHAM and her husband are members of Christian Fellowship Center in Baton Rouge, Louisiana. Don is an inspector for the Exxon Oil Company. They have three children. Betty Dale and her husband, Hal Westlund, live in Huntington Beach, California; sons, Russ and Darrell, and their families live in Baton Rouge, Louisiana.

How Good To Be Free!

By Dorothy Boyd

as told to Quin Sherrer

As my husband, Ronnie, shaved, he whistled a chorus that had begun to drive me up the walls. For the fifth straight morning, while I showered at the other end of the bathroom, I clamped a washrag between my teeth to keep from screaming at him.

"Dear God," I questioned silently as I stared at the blue tile wall, "does Ronnie have to be so happy all the time? It just doesn't seem normal."

I never heard an answer. I was carrying on a one-way conversation with God anyway.

For fourteen years Ronnie had pushed books at me, trying to make me become a Baptist. Each night, in turn, I had prayed silently that he would become a Catholic.

Now we had reached an impasse. A few weeks earlier he had boldly announced that Jesus had baptized him in His Holy Spirit. Suddenly he was hungrily reading his Bible, singing little Gospel songs around the house and shoving more books at me.

He had changed. He was too happy. He had a new compassion and concern for other people. One of the first things I noticed that was different was the way he invited other businessmen to lunch — not to line them up for the chamber of commerce but to introduce them to Jesus.

I liked many of the changes. But it began to bug me the way he'd sit in his black recliner and read the Bible for hours. It seemed to me as though he read it all the time when he was home.

We had gotten along pretty well at home until this time. Ronnie had always been active in his church and I, in mine. But now the atmosphere around our home was becoming hostile, at least on my part.

Who did he think he was anyway, trying to shove his new experience off on me? Trying to make me be as joyful all the time as he seemed to be? Why didn't he let me alone?

I was a good Christian. I had always attended church. I said my prayers every morning and night. I taught a religion course on Saturdays, and sometimes I read the Bible.

Of course I'd glance at my watch quite often to be sure my self-allotted time for Bible teaching was up so I could place the Bible back on the coffee table where it belonged.

Over and over I tried to convince myself I had all the dimension to my Christian life I needed. Yet I realized my life was no different from any of my non-church-going friends. I didn't bother to tell anyone about Christ. I didn't think anyone would be interested. But I didn't mind telling people about our social sorority or about our school PTA program.

As Indian summer drew to a brilliant close in October, the cold war set in at our house. By the time the first azaleas budded in late January, my husband and I had hit a stalemate in our relationship.

The books Ronnie left scattered around for me to read had just gathered dust. All but one. On a nippy winter evening I sneaked off to bed early to read *Keys to Triumphant Living* by Jack Taylor. It made sense. By surrendering your whole life to Jesus, by making Him Lord of everything, He would send the Holy Spirit to give you guidance and new power.

It struck a note in my heart, more than any of the "sharing" Ronnie had tried on me. But deep down I needed to know if this was an acceptable doctrine among Roman Catholics too. Were there also people of my faith who had had their lives changed through the infilling of the Holy Spirit?

About this time Ronnie realized he needed advice on how to handle me. He went to his minister, admitting to him after four months of prodding that he knew he could not inject the Holy Spirit into my life by book-pushing or any other method.

Wisely, his minister advised him to release me to God.

Later Ronnie told me he had prayed: "God, I give up. If You

52

are going to baptize my wife in Your Holy Spirit, do it in Your own time — six months, a year, five years. I won't keep trying to do it anymore. I can't."

When my husband released me, God began to move in my life in swift fashion.

Two days later I received in the mail a pamphlet listing numerous pieces of Catholic literature. I started looking through it, planning to pick out books I could use in teaching my religion class.

Suddenly my eyes were drawn to an advertisement on a book, *Threshold of God's Promise.* The ad said it told, among other things, how some Catholics at Notre Dame University had been filled with the Holy Spirit and their lives had been turned upside down.

I ordered the book, not for my class, but for my own personal reading. Two weeks later I had a terribly sore throat and cough and made an appointment with the doctor for an examination. On the way to his office, I checked the mail box and the Catholic book I had ordered was there.

The doctor said I was on the verge of pneumonia, and he sent me to bed for at least five days. I later felt the Lord picked out the book for me, had it arrive at the time He wanted me to have it, and put me to bed so I would have to read it.

I read that little book over and over, trying to absorb everything it said. It sent me searching the Bible for answers I needed concerning the Holy Spirit's guidance. I truly believed this was an experience today's Christians should seek.

On Saturday afternoon, I was able to sit up. My husband had taken our daughters shopping and to the movies. I sprawled out on the couch in the living room and began talking to God. For five hours I prayed, in everyday simple conversation, pouring out my heart to God.

Though I was praying for forgiveness, I once blurted out, "But, Lord, I know I'm as good as Ronnie." At that moment, I felt such a conviction for my spiritual pride, I cried out, "Oh, Lord, forgive me."

I began to ask forgiveness for everything I could remember. Then I asked Him to baptize me in His Holy Spirit.

I was so wrapped in the love of Jesus, I wanted to stay enfolded in His arms forever. It was like the day I got married, had my first baby placed in my arms, enjoyed the best Christmas ever — all rolled into one.

On Monday I walked outside for the first time in a week. The pink azaleas on the north side of the house were blooming, reminding me of my own blossoming. I felt the whole world was newborn. I wanted to rush up and down the street telling everyone about Jesus, the Lord of my life.

I began to read the Bible as much as my husband had. Now I was underscoring passages which spoke to me. Imagine me marking in a Bible I had mostly displayed for years!

Soon after my new commitment, the Lord gave me courage to stand before more than 1,000 people in a Baptist church and share how He had touched my life and had drawn my husband and me closer together. Never in my wildest dreams could I have imagined a quiet Catholic like myself having the boldness to stand before a Baptist congregation. The Holy Spirit guided me all the way.

My husband and I can actually talk about religion now. We even pray together daily. We have started a Bible study group at our home which meets every Monday evening.

Sometimes as many as fifteen people crowd into the den as we study about the Holy Spirit as revealed in the Bible. Many people have come into the fullness of the Holy Spirit as they, too, have sought a deeper spiritual dimension.

On Sundays I teach a religion course to eighth-grade children at Holy Spirit Catholic Church and my husband teaches a class on how to be filled with the Holy Spirit at Park Avenue Baptist Church.

We like to share what we have found to help other married couples to avoid some of our pitfalls. When we speak before groups we urge, "Don't try to change your partner, no matter how badly you want him to share your new joy. When you release your partner to God and let Him work in His own way, in His own time, you will see far better results than anything you could have plotted. Don't bind your spouse to your wishes."

Now when Ronnie sings a chorus while he shaves, my voice from the shower harmonizes right along with him.

DOROTHY (Mrs. Ronald) BOYD, her husband and their two daughters, Holly Ann (15) and Sheri Elizabeth (13), live in Titusville, Florida. Dorothy is a member of the Holy Spirit Catholic Church in Mins, Florida. Ronald is a banker and teaches at the Park Avenue Baptist Church.

Why I Pray In The Spirit

By Jo Anne Sekowsky

One summer afternoon I remember asking the Lord to keep all outside distractions from interrupting my prayers. I began to pray in English, but a few minutes later my thoughts zeroed in on some children playing in the street outside my window.

So absorbed did I become in their activities that for several minutes I completely forgot my prayers. When I came back to myself I found I was still praying, but instead of being in English, the words were in my Spirit language (speaking in other tongues).

The Lord had indeed answered my prayer but, as He so often does, He had answered in a way that was much better than that which I had in mind.

Through this little incident, the Lord has taught me several very important things about this wonderful avenue of prayer that is open to all Spirit-baptized Christians.

Formerly I had used my Spirit language almost entirely as a language of praise, and each day I tried to set aside a few minutes to pray in the Spirit. After all, didn't Paul say, *"He that speaketh in an unknown tongue edifieth himself (helps himself grow spiritually)"? (1 Cor. 14:4).* And I knew I wanted and needed that!

But that particular day the Holy Spirit, my teacher, began to show that my Spirit language is not something to be hoarded or saved for "special occasions." Spiritually, it is my native tongue, and I saw that I should use it more and more frequently until I at least approached the biblical injunction to "pray without ceasing."

Now whenever I read or hear someone say he prays in his tongue only now and then I want to say, "Hey, you're cheating yourself. This language is for real. The more you use it, the more precious and useful and self-edifying it will become to you."

If you're at all like I am, your prayer life in English probably leaves much to be desired. Now, I know there are prayer giants, but I'm not one of them, nor are most of the people I meet. And whether I'm praying for myself, or for someone else, there are far too many "vain repetitions" and too many unknown quantities when praying for other people's needs. Worst of all, there's the reoccurring problem of not always feeling like praying.

Here's where the Holy Spirit comes in. He is the one who not only knows my needs, but those of anyone for whom I might pray, and it is He who gives me the right words, and yes, even the fervor when I pray in the Spirit. *"For if I pray in an unknown tongue, my spirit prayeth" (1 Cor. 14:14).*

Since that summer afternoon the Holy Spirit has shown me many times and on many occasions that praying in the Spirit is more fruitful than praying in English. May I share a few thoughts with you?

... when I pray for someone whose real needs I don't know, whether it's a friend or stranger, I pray in the Spirit;

... when I've reached the end of my rope over a problem and I've used up all the English words I know, but the problem still needs prayer, I pray in the Spirit;

... when I become angry, resentful or embroiled in any one of a hundred different emotions that I know are displeasing to the Lord, and yet I'm not completely able to surrender the situation to Him, I pray in the Spirit;

... when the stereo or radio is going full blast with my teen-agers' music, instead of going out of my tree, I sing along in the Spirit (no one knows the difference anyway);

... when I have to wait for someone or something, I pray in the Spirit (Did you know that even though praying in the Spirit is called "tongues" you can mentally pray in the Spirit?);

... when I'm driving or walking or shopping or doing housework or not doing anything else special, I pray in the Spirit;

... when I'm too distracted
    or

too nervous

or

too upset to concentrate in English, I pray in the Spirit.

And increasingly, each time I do, I draw closer to my Lord, and I am blessed and edified and refreshed.

Praise the Lord for " . . . *He hath put a new song in my mouth" (Ps. 40:3).*

JO ANNE SEKOWSKY (Mrs.) is the mother of two daughters, a free-lance writer and currently teaches English and journalism at Edmonds High School, Edmonds, Washington. Jo Anne is a member of St. Luke's Episcopal Church in Seattle. Jo Anne's book, A CHRISTIAN ROAD MAP FOR WOMEN TRAVELING ALONE, is a best-seller of Aglow Publications.

Great Is God's Love

By Alice Wikene

I accepted Christ as my personal Savior as a child in a Baptist church which we attended near our home. My father was a very stern person and preached the "fear of God" to us. However, I knew there was something missing in my Christian life, although there was always a strong drawing towards the church. By the time I was a teen-ager, I grew farther away from the church even though I did continue attending every evening service.

I met and married a man who was an unbeliever. But he was from a Lutheran background, and so we were married in a Lutheran church, and our two sons were baptized in this same Lutheran church, I was not in a right relationship with God during this time, nor was I trying to live my life for Him. But in His love and grace God started moving me and stirring my heart.

John and I lived in Canada and were greatly influenced by our many unsaved relatives. I feel it was God's hand that moved us to the United States in 1957. We immediately enrolled the children in Sunday school at the nearest Lutheran church, and I began attending church regularly. My faith grew and I became, once again, an openly-confessing Christian.

There were no Christians to fellowship with where I worked, and God knew my need. In His love He provided me with employment with another company in the same profession and very close to home. Now I had several Christians to share with daily. It was

59

at this time that our youngest son, Barry, was struck down by a car. The accident caused a deformity, but God healed him.

Four years later Barry and my husband were in a terrible automobile accident in Canada, which took the lives of three people, my husband's mother, his nephew and a passenger in the other car. My son suffered a serious hip injury, and my husband was not expected to live.

The most critical injury that John suffered was the head concussion which put him in a coma. His collar bone was broken, and several ribs were snapped off at the spine. One rib had punctured a lung, a kidney was damaged and his chest cage was ripped. The doctors said there was nothing they could do for him.

I was at home in Lynnwood, Washington, when I received word of the accident. My prayer was simply, "God, if You spare John's life I pray that You will make his life purposeful. I'll accept whatever You have in store for me." I asked God for strength for whatever would be necessary. God gave me strength beyond all understanding, and peace. I had a long drive ahead of me up to British Columbia, but God sustained me as I drove all night.

When I saw my husband, who was still in a deep coma, I took his hand between my hands and told him, "I love you." He miraculously opened his mouth and spoke of his love for me. He was still in the coma. God acknowledged his love, honored my heartfelt prayer, and spared John's life. John did not come out of the coma until two days later. Many Christians prayed for us during this time and these prayers were answered.

I brought John and Barry back to a hospital in Seattle. The doctors were able to help Barry's condition through surgery. John had brain specialists and bone specialists and internal specialists, but little could be done for him medically.

John was constantly in great discomfort and suffered continual pain from his badly broken and damaged body. There was no position in which he could even sleep to avoid the back pain. Several months after the accident the doctors said that the way John was then was how he would be for the rest of his life. I could not accept this statement. I was determined to find relief and healing for my husband. My faith in God continued to grow and along with it, hope.

One day I called a friend, Joline Erickson, to pray with me over the phone for a particular need. During our conversation I confided in her that I was really hungering and thirsting for more of Jesus. She was very understanding since she had recently been that way too. Then she enthusiastically shared with me that she had found the answer. She quoted several Bible verses. I wrote them down and later looked each one up in the Bible and meditated upon it.

All the verses were on the baptism in the Holy Spirit. I had not heard of this before. So I went to God in prayer, acknowledging that I knew nothing about it but I could see it was spoken of in the Bible. "If it is for me, God," I prayed, "I want You to baptize me in the Holy Spirit." I told no one of my prayer; it was between God and me.

Two days later, at the service in my Lutheran church, I went to the altar for consecration. The very moment hands touched me and the prayers began, I received the baptism in the Holy Spirit. For me, this was the greatest single experience in my Christian life. The Bible suddenly became completely alive and I couldn't put it down. Love poured out of me like rivers of living water. People who I had known for years and even casual acquaintances alike noticed a difference and asked what had happened to me.

During the same church service Joline slipped me a book on how to speak in tongues. I didn't know anything about this either, but I prayed about it. I was all alone, having my private devotions, when God gave me a beautiful heavenly language. This was the first time in my life I'd ever heard a tongue, and it was my very own. I could hardly wait to tell Joline and, of course, she rejoiced with me.

I shared my experience with my husband. He was very attentive and deeply interested. During the past years I had been praying for my husband's salvation and had lived by 1 Peter 3:1, *"Likewise, ye wives, be in subjection to your own husbands; that, if any obey not the word, they also may without the word be won by the conversation [conduct] of the wives."* God answered this prayer; John was saved. He also wanted the baptism in the Holy Spirit. But he didn't receive it immediately.

One evening in our home about eighteen months after the accident, we, Joline and Marvin Erickson and Isabel Huntoon were having a Bible study. We always spent much time in prayer. We laid hands on John and prayed and anointed him with oil, according to the Scriptures, and immediately he received a miracle healing from God and was made whole. Praise God! A short time later, on the same evening, he received the baptism in the Holy Spirit.

When God healed John all pain left him completely and his arms shot straight up in the air, something he had been unable to do since the accident. In fact, he had not been able to raise his arms above his shoulders because of the broken collar bone that had healed improperly and the snapped-off ribs.

Jesus saved me and baptized me in the Holy Spirit! He also healed me and He healed my husband! God protects me too; I have not spent one full day in bed in over fifteen years.

God has removed all of the Christians with whom I fellowshiped from around me at my job. But now I am able to stand alone with His help and not topple over. I can witness with boldness now just as the Scriptures said I would. Jesus is so real and strong within me; I can't stop praising Him. The baptism in the Holy Spirit, as the Bible describes in Acts 2:17 . . . *"And it shall come to pass in the last days, saith God, I will pour out of my Spirit upon all flesh . . . "* truly filled the void in my life. Praise God!

ALICE (Mrs. John) WIKENE is a member of the Gospel Lighthouse in Lynnwood, Washington. John and Alice have two grown sons and a granddaughter. Alice has been a professional photoengraver and mitographer with the John Fluke Manufacturing Company, an electronics firm. The Wikenes have their home open at all times to Christian groups.

Happiness Is Jesus

By Lee Perry

My water baptism in the Baptist church just after I had been saved at the age of nine was a memorable occasion. I wore my best dress, a white organdy one. As I was buried to my sins and lifted up, I noticed that my dress was wilted, but I didn't care, for I rose to a new victorious life in Jesus Christ.

I dearly loved the church and its activities. When the church doors were open my family and I were there. But as a young teen-ager, realizing that my father was making me go, I decided that I would someday go only as often as I pleased. God allowed me that privilege.

I was married in the Methodist church and remained a Methodist for eleven years before going back into the Baptist church. After my first child was born, I once again became serious about my church attendance. After my second child was born, I slipped a disc. My doctor said that I was within ten or twelve days from surgery. This was the turning point in my life. I had plenty of time to lie in God's green pastures and think. I promised God that in return for my healing I would serve Him better. He did heal me and led me into paths before unknown to me.

After my fourth child was born, I took the children and once again joined a Baptist church. By this time I felt that we were spiritually starved; yet my husband refused to come with me. I was torn emotionally between my husband's desires and wanting more of the Lord. I plunged into Bible courses which were offered in my new church. I could not understand why I could feel the presence of the Holy Spirit so completely sometimes when at other times He seemed far away.

In my spiritual hunger I took courses in Old Testament, New Testament, teacher development and anything that was being offered. God was fulfilling much of my need for spiritual bread. More and more, my husband began resenting my denomination and anything I would say about the Lord or His Word. I trembled when my husband walked in while I was reading the Bible. Mistakenly he came to believe that anything I said about the Lord or my church was criticism of him and his church. Therefore, I learned to be quiet. I learned never to put the church before my family so that it could ever be said that I neglected them.

Throughout the years I kept myself very busy. I took courses in dressmaking, drapery making, ceramics, decoupage, horticulture and interior designing. I did all the yard work, housework, cooking, painting, and much of the repair work. I tried to do all the things which needed to be done. When we bought a large home I planted all the shrubs and grass, made many of the draperies, refinished and antiqued furniture, planted and maintained a vegetable garden and continued raising four children.

I became exhausted. I felt that none of my family cared about helping with the work and care of our home. It was at this time that I needed God so desperately that I read the Bible completely through in two months. Two Scriptures especially were a great source of strength to me. One was Jeremiah 29:13, *"And ye shall seek me, and find me, when ye shall search for me with all your heart."* The other was Jeremiah 33:3, *"Call unto me, and I will answer thee, and shew thee great and mighty things, which thou knowest not."*

I had to cross this deep valley before I could ever find God in completeness. Often in my physical exhaustion and despair I felt as though I were sinking into the miry clay. Then, I would look up and see the light to lighten my way, until the feeling of aloneness came again.

Then one day I looked up and cried, "Oh God, it is Your way and Your will I want and never again my will." At that moment, on bended knees beside my bed, I saw a rushing ball of light. Whirling, it came faster and faster until it was directly before me and then enveloped my very being. I felt the Spirit as never before and I began sobbing, rejoicing, and praising my wonderful Lord all at once. From that time on my life was transformed. No longer did I have bitterness and resentfulness in my heart, and new strength rose within me. I was free!

Jesus made me free from the chains and shackles which had bound me. I had, at long last, given all of myself to Him and He truly set me free. Never was I happier; never was I more at peace; never did I have so much love for my Lord and for others; never did I have more strength; never was I more free! He lives, He lives, He lives within my heart!

In my search for God, I had read *God's Smuggler, The Cross and The Switchblade,* and *They Speak with Other Tongues,* among other books. I knew that it was true that God performed such miracles in the lives of His children. I asked Him to reveal Himself to me in the same way, and He has. He continues to guide and teach me each day.

About two weeks after I had surrendered my will to the Lord and was crucified to self, I asked God to also give me the heavenly language I had heard about. I wanted all of God's goodness and gifts that He was willing to give me. I knelt beside my bed and opened my mouth and God's gift of the heavenly language poured forth. Again I was crying and praising God. For two days I sang and praised God in this manner and only stopped in the presence of my family. I had never before heard anyone speak in tongues, but I knew it to be a reality.

I had surrendered all of myself to God. It was no longer I that lived, but Christ within me. The difference in being a superficial Christian and a Spirit-filled Christian is tremendous! I had often felt the Holy Spirit before on special occasions but now the Holy Spirit's presence is ever present and His great power is prevailing.

There is no worry in my life anymore but peace in its stead. Yes, I am greatly burdened at times, but it is for others, and I pray for them until I feel the peace of God and know that He is answering. Never before had I cared about and loved others as I do now. God has placed so many precious ones in my pathway to minister to, to love, to pray for, and to show them that the master of their lives cares for them.

Now God provides all the time it takes for me to spend time with His children, even those who do not know Him. I constantly find myself praising God while driving along the streets, doing household duties or whatever is required of me. It pleases me so to awake at night and find I'm praising my Lord, for I know my love for Him is constant.

Jesus truly said, *"What things soever ye desire, when ye pray, believe that ye receive them, and ye shall have them"* *(Mark 11:24).*

LEE (Mrs. James) PERRY is a member of and teaches at First Baptist Church in Dallas, Texas. Her husband is a president of an insurance company. They have four children: Jim Jr. (23), Tom (20), Carol (17) and Bob (14).

His Love Overflowing

By Alice Brown

Growing up in a Montana Indian reservation just a few miles from a national wilderness area, I knew our pastor mainly as the man who came over in faded blue jeans with the back pockets ripped off to plan big game hunts with the men in our family. The biggest event of the year was the opening of hunting season.

I looked forward to the day I would be big enough to go along. Finally, that day arrived, and with a 30-30 that seemed as big as I was, I waded out into the waist-deep fresh snow — right behind the preacher. Every third step I tripped over something hidden under the snow, and fell flat on my face. But determined to keep up, I picked myself up and trudged on, getting wetter all the time. Somehow, it became a parable of things to come.

When I enrolled in college, the professors and instructors seemed intent upon impressing us of our gross ignorance and naivete about the world we lived in. Determined to show them I wasn't all that naive and ignorant, I delved into books of every subject with vigor. We had a newly-founded Wesley House on campus for Methodist students with worship each morning. lectures, and seminars. I took all the seminars in which we studied the writings of all the popular theologians of the day and became a great debater. I rarely let our campus minister say two sentences without contesting him and questioning his statements. But in my heart I knew there was a great void. I knew I didn't have the answers that were really satisfying — all I had were questions.

One night I happened to pick up my Bible (which was not my habit), and I opened it to Matthew 7:7, *"Ask, and it shall be given you; seek, and you shall find; knock, and it shall be opened unto you."* I began to weep uncontrollably and didn't understand why. I knew there was something I needed to receive that I wasn't receiving, but I didn't know what it was. I mentioned this experience to my friends and to several clergymen, but none could help me.

In the meantime, I went on making intellectual attainment my god, debating everything and anything — always questioning. I left the Wesley fellowship and began attending the Unitarian church because their service usually consisted of reporting upon and debating social issues of the day, and I liked to think I was intellectually involved with what was going on in the world.

Dick, my fiance, had continued living at the Wesley house three years, rebelling totally against their program, but God had His hand upon our lives even in those rebellious years. We were married as soon as I graduated and after two years in Washington, D.C., were transferred to southern California. There we joined a church in which we had "encounter groups" and "sensitivity groups." The encounter groups generally turned into a debate time over theology and I was right there, contesting our minister at every turn. After the sermons, we had a "talk back," and I always went with my intellectual gun loaded, right behind the minister, determined to keep up. The truth was that if someone had asked me what book in the New Testament followed Acts, I wouldn't have known, and I knew even less about the Old Testament.

Then I applied to teach first grade in an "economically deprived" area of Los Angeles county. I knew absolutely nothing about reaching first graders, and I soon found out that the children were not impressed with a display of my intellect. One boy sat each day with the same filthy ski jacket pulled over his head while another at any odd moment would jump up and begin screaming and running around the room. I knew what they needed was love. My heart ached as it never had before because I didn't have any love to give them.

Again I saw how limited I was when our new associate pastor had terminal cancer. Someone called and asked if I would join a 24-hour prayer chain for him. Wanting to be agreeable, I took the

5-6 a.m. hour. After five minutes I was totally bored and wondered how to spend the rest of the hour. All my intellectual debates hadn't taught me what to do now. How did I talk with this God?

Once more I had to face my inadequacies when our church set up a week's camp in a minority area for crafts and art work for the neighborhood children. At the end of the week, I was putting all the crafts of the children into shoe boxes for them to take home when one little girl came up to me and asked, "What kind of camp was this anyway?" I looked down at her shoe box and I knew I was just another face that drifted into her life for one week. A voice inside said, "All you have given her of Me, Alice, can be fitted into that shoe box. I'm bigger than that."

Suddenly it was clear that debating religion had done nothing for me, had given me nothing to give others, had left me only with a void. I made a decision to seek a more Christian life.

The next day one of my close friends in the church, Louise, came up with a bubbling joy that was new. She had so many problems. I knew her problems — nothing had changed, yet all of a sudden she was radiant. She said, "Alice, you have to come with me sometime to this other church." She had gone to Anaheim Christian Center and Evangelist Dick Mills had given her Isaiah 43:18-19: *"Remember ye not the former things, neither consider the things of old. Behold, I will do a new thing; now it shall spring forth; shall ye not know it? I will even make a way in the wilderness, and rivers in the desert."* I couldn't understand how one Scripture could make anyone so happy, but it was for me too.

Another friend said, "Oh, I have a Presbyterian friend who goes there on Thursday mornings to their prayer and share. She says if you want the full impact of it, you have to go forward to pray with people."

The next Thursday I was there, and I could feel the joy in the people around me. It was so real. When the pastor gave the invitation to go forward to pray for others, I was the first to go "to get the full impact of it all." There before me was a Canadian businessman with unbelievable physical and financial problems. He looked at me with total trust and faith that when I laid hands on him, he would be completely healed. Gingerly, I laid hands on his head and prayed, "Oh, God, what have I gotten myself into — Jesus, help me now!" Suddenly, a power went through my body like a large electrical current. Stunned, I could only stand with my mouth open.

The pastor, Ralph Wilkerson, spun around to me in that instant and asked, "And what do you need from God?"

Still numb, I shook my head with my mouth hanging open. As I left the church, a voice inside said, "It's not what you need from Me, Alice, but what I need from you."

I went home and for days devoured all the New Testament but still didn't understand. After four attempts in which I cancelled out, I finally got together enough nerve to talk with Pastor Wilkerson. I told him about everything that had happened up to that point and he just smiled and said, "You want more of Jesus."

At the time I thought, "Oh, brother, that's about as much of an over-simplification as one can get." But he was right. Second Corinthians 11:3 says, *"But I fear, lest by any means, as the serpent beguiled Eve through his subtilty, so your minds should be corrupted from the simplicity that is in Christ."* Pastor Wilkerson put me in a room with a tape about an experience called the baptism in the Holy Spirit. I had never heard of such a thing. I took notes but understood little.

Then a woman came in and asked me if I'd like to pray. She prayed softly with me in a language I'd never heard before. I listened, fascinated. It was beautiful and I sensed she was praying for me and that she was very earnest. She finally stood up and gave me her address and phone number and told me to call her any time.

That night I wanted to go to an all-night prayer meeting the Christian Center has having prior to their charismatic clinic. Dick said, "No, I'm not going to have you driving alone in the middle of the night, but no one is stopping you from praying in the bedroom."

Still puzzled by the experience of that Thursday morning, I began to pray about it and reenacted it in my mind. Except this time as I watched myself reach out to lay hands on the man, I looked down at my hands and saw instead the nailscarred hands that belong to Jesus, and inside me I heard that same voice say, "You see, Alice, when you pray in My name, your hands become an extension of My hands."

The revelation was so overwhelming that I could hear myself praising God in a new language I had never heard. Yet I didn't know how to make a sound. It was such a holy moment. In the presence of the Lord, I saw myself in comparison to His holiness and knew how unworthy I was of His love. Isaiah 6:5 was later to have much meaning to me.

At the time I didn't pray a prayer of confession of my sins because I didn't know I was supposed to, but I thank God He looks upon our hearts. A week later I received a release to praise God freely in this new beautiful language which He gives to praise Him in. It is completely at the control of my will to praise Him in this language.

But that was just the beginning of God's taming of my unruly nature to conform me into His image and to make me into the wife and mother He wants me to be. Soon after, Dick received the Lord and a year later received the baptism in the Holy Spirit. After three years of walking with the Lord I realized, when we moved to Texas, how much God had been at work in our lives.

When we moved in, we were beseiged by neighborhood children who thought a new baby in the neighborhood was a great novelty.

Often at night when we'd lay hands on our baby and pray, we'd turn around and find five or six neighbor children in the room praying also. The same was true when we'd kneel and pray with our three-year-old girl.

Soon, three of the children received Jesus into their hearts by asking questions about what they had experienced in our home. They brought back six other friends, all of whom have received the Lord Jesus and we began a neighborhood Bible study for the children.

One evening, when the children had all left, it suddenly occurred to me that I did have something to give now. I thanked God for those first graders and the children in the crafts programs who had made me feel my need to receive Jesus that I might now have His love flowing through me and even going out to others.

ALICE (Mrs. Richard) BROWN and her family are currently living in Pine Bluff, Arkansas. Their children are Laura and Patrick. Alice and Dick both graduated from the University of Montana. Alice has written an Aglow Bible Study, PATTERNS FOR PARENTS.

Love, Or Else!

By Martha Banks

Christ's command to love seemed to jump out at me every time I opened the Bible. "Love — or else!" He seemed to say. "Love or go to hell. Take your pick."

I felt that I had not loved people freely since I was five or six years old. On my next birthday I would be fifty, just a harmless housewife with a faithful husband and a fine son in college. Yet maybe I was failing in the one thing Christians are supposed to do.

I tried so hard, so terribly hard to please people. I didn't quarrel; I kept the dog fenced in and the TV turned low; I sent birthday greetings and get-well cards. I weighed every word I said, trying to say the right thing, trying not to offend anyone in any way. Yet something kept telling me that this wasn't love.

My face was tired from smiling when I didn't really mean it. My heart was full of resentment from pretending I agreed with people when I really didn't. Worst of all, it seemed that I was alone and smothering in a heavy, invisible cocoon. The world was "out there," and I could see and hear it and go through all the motions of response without being able to reach out and touch people.

"Lord, what can I do? You told us to love. You said love is the most important thing we do in life. But I don't know how. I love Dave and Davey and our folks, but I feel so pinched and shriveled inside. What can I do?"

I thought the Lord was disgusted with me because it seemed He wasn't even bothering to listen to me.

This was the state I was in when Mom, 73, fell and broke her wrist on October 12, 1972.

Dad, 76, came and stayed with us, and when Mom was released from the hospital a few days later she joined us. I was so glad to have them, yet my pleasure, as always, was mixed with unbearable anxiety.

I was extremely anxious to please them, extremely anxious for them to be comfortable and happy. I was constantly alert for some sign that I was failing them, or that they were disappointed in me. Out of the corner of my eye I watched to see whether they cleaned up their plates or toyed with their food. I listened to the inflection of their voices, weighing the meaning in every change. At night I lay awake, worrying for fear they weren't sleeping well. Every moment of every day I was looking for, expecting, and finding signals of their discontent. Then I would try harder than ever to be a "good daughter."

My nerves were tight, and my skin felt stretched across the bones of my face. My throat ached painfully and my chest hurt, as though someone were standing on my chest, with both hands gripping my throat.

I was ashamed to complain to our family doctor, but I wrote him a letter, and he gave me a prescription for tranquilizers. The pills eliminated the strangling sensation but they didn't touch the part of me that hurt the most.

Mom and Dad were obviously miserable. They were as uptight as I was. While they didn't complain about anything, they stayed holed up in their bedroom most of the time, said polite things about the food but didn't eat much, and talked to each other in hushed voices.

The tranquilizers kept me from crying, but I was feeling desperate. Every morning I prayed, "Oh, Lord, please give me the gift of the Holy Spirit just for today so I can love the way You want me to." Spiritually impoverished, I was begging for just enough nourishment to survive.

Originally an Episcopalian, I had turned Roman Catholic when I was 38. When I was 13, I was confirmed by Bishop Mann, and when I was 39, I was confirmed again by Bishop John Wright. On both occasions I was told the Holy Spirit would strengthen me to live a Christian life, but both times I somehow got the impression that the power was stowed away for times of emergency — something like a fire extinguisher.

Early in 1972, Mom stumbled over a copy of Kevin Ranaghan's book, *Catholic Pentecostals,* and a few weeks later someone mailed me a copy of George Stockhowe's *Jesus Is Alive.* Reading them, I was impressed by the fact that, for some people, the power was active in their everyday lives; it was not labeled, "In case you are burned at the stake — break this glass."

By October I was so concerned over my invisible shroud that I was really afraid I would go to hell. No efforts of mine had succeeded in breaking that shell. But now I was wondering rather hopefully, "Could the baptism in the Holy Spirit help me?"

Everyday from the middle of October until November 12, I prayed for just enough of the Holy Spirit to keep me going. Not knowing enough to pray, "Fill me up!" I just asked for a beggar's share. And since I couldn't perceive any difference in myself I thought the Lord didn't want to give me even His crumbs.

On Sunday, November 12, when my husband, Dave, our twenty-year-old son, Davey, and I came home from church we found Mom and Dad waiting with their coats on, their belongings packed in suitcases and brown paper bags.

"We want to go home," Mom said.

"Oh! Why? We thought you would be staying for another month at least." I was shocked and disappointed.

"We want to go home now," Mom pleaded.

We piled their belongings into the car, tucked Mom and Dad into the front seat and Dave drove them home.

I closed the front door and cried. To think that I was so unloving that my own parents couldn't stand to live in the same house with me!

"If I had loved them enough they would have stayed," I reasoned.

Just three days before Mom fell I had learned that a charismatic group was meeting on Sunday nights at St. Thomas Episcopal Church in Oakmont, the parish church in which I had grown up. So, as soon as Dave got home from taking my folks to their place, I said, "Let's go to that prayer and praise thing at St. Thomas tonight." I thought maybe, just maybe, if a whole lot of people prayed with me the Lord might listen.

I really didn't know what to expect or how to behave. It was a cultural shock to hear guitars and a tambourine and handclapping in that familiar old Gothic church, but I loved all of it. When we sang, and the others put their hands up in the air, I put mine up just a little bitty bit, but I was wishing I had the courage to put them all the way up.

Then everyone knelt and started praying softly. I summoned all of my courage and cried out, "Lord, please give me the gift of the Holy Spirit so I can love!"

There was a long, long silence. I was horribly embarrassed. Bitter tears streamed down my cheeks. I had humbled myself to cry out for His help in front of all these people, and still He wouldn't pay attention to me. My heart felt broken.

Then the woman who had been playing the guitar came and said gently, "Marcie, would you like us to pray with you?"

"Yes, please."

A nice looking young fellow asked me if I loved Jesus, and I said, "Yes."

"Do you renounce everything pertaining to the occult, including astrology, Edgar Cayce and Jeanne Dixon?"

I wanted to say, "I renounced all that years ago," but I didn't want to sound argumentative so I just said, "Yes."

Then they put their hands on me and prayed. They prayed and prayed, but nothing happened. At last they stopped praying, and they hugged and kissed me. I was grateful to them, but I didn't think Jesus had given me His Holy Spirit because I didn't feel any joy or speak in tongues. Another fellow grinned and said, "Take this home and read it." It was James Beall's *School of the Holy Spirit.*

The next morning after Dave and Davey left, I read a few chapters of the Bible and started the first chapter of Beall's book.

At 9 a.m. I was reading page 13, a paraphrase of the Apostles' Creed. As I read I was mentally agreeing with each phrase. The last phrase was, " . . . deliberately pours out His Holy Spirit."

As I finished reading those words it seemed that someone lifted me out of my chair. My arms went high into the air, and I was singing a long and beautiful hymn in a very strange language. Jesus had touched me.

In those few minutes I realized for the first time that God loves me — that He really knows me, and really, really loves me!

It was so beautiful, so shockingly beautiful that I was crying and laughing and saying, "Oh, thank You! Thank You!" over and over again.

The realization that God loves me just as I am, even with all the unloveliness in my heart, was all that I needed to begin to truly love others.

The Holy Spirit began moving so swiftly in my life that I could hardly believe it. I found myself hugging and kissing people with genuine affection, and I marveled at how wonderful they were. Suddenly I could converse with people, strangers, even my parents, without the old stiffness and self-consciousness. I could say what was on my mind. And I was interested in every little detail in the lives of others. Whether they were happy or troubled, I felt for them; I reached out to them, and we touched.

My smile didn't feel pasted on any more. The cocoon was broken. I was free, free to love as Jesus wants me to. In addition, Dave received the baptism in the Holy Spirit the same night as I did, and Davey asked for it the following week. Four months later Mom and Dad received it, and that May all five of us attended the Greater Pittsburgh Charismatic Conference.

The Holy Spirit continues to help me daily to do what I cannot do alone: to love others as Jesus has loved me.

MARTHA (Mrs. David) BANKS and her family live in Pittsburgh, Pennsylvania, where David is senior patent engineer in the law department of Gulf Oil Corporation. The Banks have a son, David, who is 22. The Banks now attend St. Thomas Episcopal Church in Oakmont, Pennsylvania.

Second Chance From God

By Rita Reed Bennett

The audience of young people was very attentive as Don Underwood, a Christian disc jockey in Seattle, Washington, began his talk. "I had always lived to please myself," he said seriously, "really caring for no one else. It didn't matter who I walked on, just as long as 'number one' was taken care of. I was a wretched person and desperately wicked . . . then at the age of nine I was converted to Jesus Christ!" After a moment of total silence the young people burst into laughter . . . because everybody knows that a nine year old couldn't be *that* bad . . . or could he?

What Don said is true of all unconverted mankind. You and I have been sinful* and self-centered because we were born dead at the very core. Hard as it is to believe this when we look at a sweet baby, it becomes easier when the child is in the "terrible two's." One of his favorite words is "mine," and a playmate may receive a crack on the head when "my" toy is retrieved. We still might make excuses for the child, but what if, at twenty-two, he were still acting the same way? To get along in society most people learn to behave, but the condition of the heart remains the same.

A psychologist in Seattle said recently, "Any unregenerate

---

* In addition to sin being the very nature of fallen man (Ps. 51:5; Rom. 3:23), it also means choosing to go your own way instead of God's way (Isa. 53:6). God's way is Jesus Christ (John 14:6) and Jesus, Himself, taught that the world would be reproved of sin because they didn't believe in Him and receive Him (John 16:8,9; John 1:12).

person is capable of doing *anything* if pushed far enough."

What caused Hitler or Stalin to order millions to their deaths? What about the terrorist activity around the world which has resulted in the murder of many innocent people? How about history in general and the cruelty of man to man?

The Bible sums it up, *"All have sinned, and come short of the glory of God . . . There is none righteous, no, not one: there is none that understandeth, there is none that seeketh after God. They are all gone out of the way, they are together become unprofitable" (Rom. 3:23; 3:10-12).*

Like the disc jockey, at the age of nine, I, too, was freed from my inherited nature and all my sins and received Jesus Christ. Shortly after, I was baptized by immersion in a full gospel church. All it took was a simple prayer of repentance and acceptance of Jesus, God's Son, into the center of my life. What a wonderful experience! The Holy Spirit had joined Himself to my spirit making me a new creature or a new creation (2 Cor. 5:17). In my child-like way I had seen Jesus to be *"God made man,"* who died in my place to take away all sin, a real person, who can be experienced here and now as well as in eternity (John 1:1-14, 14:21, Rev. 3:20). At this time I also received the baptism of the Holy Spirit but did not really understand what had happened to me.

I wish I could follow these statements up with a beautiful story of a life lived close to God from that day on. To be truthful I must confess that I sinned more after I was born into God's kingdom than I had ever done before!

It was something like the parable of the farmer who went out to sow his seed (Matt. 13:1-23). In part of Jesus' story, the seeds fell on stony places — they did germinate and sprout, but because of the shallowness of the earth they were scorched in the heat of the day. I had no root in myself or depth in Scripture because I received very little teaching to help my spiritual understanding; as a result I was an active Christian only a short time.

One of the main things that turned me off as I entered my teens was the long list of rules to follow if I was going to try to be a real Christian. Christianity was presented to me as a religion of works instead of faith!

A cartoon recently showed geologists excavating in Mount Sinai, uncovering two tablets of stone and exclaiming to one another, "Oh, no! Ten *more* commandments!" So many people—

some Christians included—look at Christianity as a long, difficult list of "thou shalt nots."

It wasn't the Ten Commandments that bothered me, but the many, many other rules which never could be located in my Bible when I looked for them years later: "Thou shalt not look stylish; thou shalt not wear lipstick; thou shalt not go to the skating rink, etc. etc." To my sad realization I found that "man-made" rules had been keeping me separated from the love of God all those years. If only someone had given me a list of "thou shalts" — something more positive to live by!

I developed a different idea about God than that which I had experienced at the age of nine. The conclusion was soon reached. "If anything is fun it must be a sin." In other words, God's first duty was to see that the world and all it had to offer was much more exciting than the Christian faith.

The result? I rebelled. I thought, "If that's what it takes to be a Christian — I'll never make it — so why even try?" I began a long struggle with misery, emptiness, confusion, and everything that goes along with walking away from God.

In 1957, my senior year at the University of Florida, my oldest brother, Bill,* realizing I was still floundering in my faith, wrote suggesting the Episcopal church as a possibility to me. Although I am not pushing a particular brand of Christianity, this church played an important part in my getting right with God. For someone else, another church might have been more helpful. I particularly appreciated the esthetic beauty of the Episcopal church — the kneeling to pray and the reverence at the Communion service. The priest at the campus chapel was a surprise to me; he was an intellectual and at the same time truly believed in God!

This was a rare combination in my academic surroundings. The attitude was generally that the two didn't go together. He didn't say much about "thou shalt nots" but instead quoted St. Augustine, who said: "Love God and do as you please." What a liberating statement! How positive — just where you are — start loving God. In time I was to find, as I loved God more and more, I naturally wanted to be doing what pleased Him. I was starting on the way back.

After receiving my bachelor of arts degree in education, in February of 1958, and teaching school for one semester, I moved

---

* Dr. William S. Reed, Christian surgeon and author.

to Newark, New Jersey, to work as an apprentice in social work. I worked in a church-state subsidized agency with emotionally damaged girls, ages five through twelve It was quite a challenging year, to say the least, and I felt a great need to be more of a channel of God's love to these children. Unfortunately the channel was clogged up most of the time.

It was during this time when I was becoming an Episcopalian that Bill wrote me a letter about confirmation. He said that this was the service in which a bishop, with the laying-on-of-hands, would pray for me to be empowered with the Holy Spirit. (I'm glad he told me, since I was expecting it to be sort of like the initiation ceremony into my sorority!)

The Second Office of instruction in the Book of Common Prayer explains that the bishop will pray for the strengthening gifts of the Holy Spirit (1 Cor. 12:7-11). I couldn't have told anyone what the gifts were or where to find them in the Bible. No wonder after the service I felt, acted, and thought exactly the same as before. Nevertheless the bishop's prayer that I would daily increase in the Holy Spirit was heard by God and answered a year and a half later.

Returning to Tampa, I taught exceptional children for one year and then went to work in child welfare for the state of Florida. During this time one Sunday as I was leaving church with my junior choir, I spotted a familiar face. It was an old friend of junior high days, Gaye Miller. We visited afterwards and I invited her to meet me at my apartment nearby. Years had passed and we had a lot of news to catch up on.

One thing in particular about Gaye was different; she began to talk about God right in broad daylight that Sunday afternoon. She spoke freely and enthusiastically of Jesus and when I asked what had happened to her, Gaye said that she had received the power of the Holy Spirit. Indeed something wonderful *had* happened to her, but because my capacity to receive was about a thimble full — I listened awhile, then changed the subject.

My friend had just moved back to Tampa so I invited her to room with me. She was a fine person to share an apartment with but used to do something I thought was a bit funny for a person in her early twenties. Every Friday night Gaye faithfully attended a home prayer meeting. I figured prayer meetings must be on the dull side and thought she should be doing some *normal* things, such as going to dances, parties, and shows.

One day, while basking on the beach the next summer, Gaye told me something more about her experience with the Holy Spirit. She said that when she was baptized in the Holy Spirit she spoke in tongues. What a shock! I remembered the "speaking in tongues" in the church of my youth. Indeed I knew that I had spoken in tongues following my conversion. The memory of it had troubled me through the years, since no one had explained what it meant or encouraged me to continue in it. Mainly what I remembered were the excesses. Gaye was too nice a girl to be involved in such things!

I looked at her clinically. "Hummm! How often do you do this?" I thought perhaps this came over her maybe four times a year, and fortunately when I was somewhere else!

"Rita, I speak in tongues *every day*," Gaye replied gently.

"But . . . I've never heard you!" I exclaimed.

Gaye made herself comfortable in the warm sand and explained more to me. "Speaking in tongues or 'speaking in the Spirit' doesn't have to be loud any more than other oral prayer has to be. It is so great to be able to speak and trust the Holy Spirit to guide your language, praying for your own needs and for the needs of others that are beyond your own human knowledge. This kind of prayer is beyond the intellect."

What a statement! In all my schooling I had been taught that there was nothing greater than the intellect. I had never heard of the triune nature of man and that the spirit, not the intellect (part of the soul), was the greatest part of regenerated man.

As she talked on, relieving my fears in this area, I made one comment, "Oh . . . I wish I could do that." Of course, the Lord Jesus was listening to our conversation!

A short time later Gaye returned to North Carolina to join with friends who had been instrumental in her walk with God. Three months later, in October 1960, I received a call from one of her relatives saying that while on her lunch hour Gaye had had a cerebral hemorrhage, lost consciousness, and eight hours later — died! What terrible news — for me. I had no doubt about where Gaye was: she was the most truly Christian person I had ever known. It was the suddenness of her death that hit me hardest.

She had no time to make things right with God, but Gaye had had no need to; she *lived* in a state of readiness.

83

What upset me most, in addition to losing my friend, was that I wasn't sure I was ready. Then, too, what if I did arrive in the heavenly kingdom someday, and there would be no one who was there because of my witness to them? As I lay back on my bed I thought of the sixteen years I had been a Christian and had never once witnessed to anyone about Jesus Christ, except one time by sheer accident.

In 1955, I had entered the Miss Tampa Beauty Contest (to my parents' consternation). Having been chosen one of the five finalists, we had come to the stage one by one and were asked three questions. The first two I answered easily.

It was the third question that stumped me. "If there is someone in this world you want to be like, who would it be?" What an easy question, but my mind drew a blank! I could think of no one I desired to be like. I had to have an answer.

I found myself saying, "There's no one in this world I want to be like but there is one in heaven — the Lord Jesus Christ." Immediately I was embarrassed by my answer. Oh, why had I pushed my beliefs off on these people? Hadn't I learned that this was not the intelligent thing to do? I could take no credit for *that* witness; it was totally unplanned. Now I began having some sleepless nights thinking about the wasted years, the mistakes of the past, and the purpose of life.

Gaye's funeral found me more upset than ever. As I was leaving after the service, I met the couple in whose home she had met for prayer each week. Several weeks later I received a telephone call from Bertha. After reintroducing herself she said, "I was praying this morning and God brought you to my heart and began to speak to me about you."

"He did?" I gulped. (I thought to myself, "I didn't know God still knew I was around.")

"Yes," she said, "and if you'd like to drop over sometime I'd like to share these things with you."

It didn't take long to think that offer over. "I'll be right there!" I quickly hung up the phone and got into my red M.G. I had never known anyone to speak so confidently and intimately about God. I really wanted to know what God had to say to me; no one had ever talked like this to me before.

I arrived at a neat, white frame house and was greeted by a motherly-looking woman in her late fifties. As I was seated in the living room she shared with me, and I had a deep inner witness to the words spoken. Bertha was sharing through the *gift of knowledge** many things about my present, and something of the future that no one but God could have revealed to her.

At that moment I decided to attend the next prayer meeting. This meant cancelling an audition to sing with a combo in a night club on the Gulf Beach. I was to drive over with several other girls and thought they might think it strange of me to choose a prayer meeting over the audition. I cancelled anyway.

That Friday, as I arrived at the meeting, the house was jammed with people; the living room, dining room and porch were full. There must have been eighty or more in attendance. One of the things that impressed me was the joyful expressions on their faces. There were people of all ages, many denominations and backgrounds. When they sang hymns and choruses they sang wholeheartedly "to the Lord." The prayers were spontaneous and certainly from the heart. After some time had elapsed the leader took me by surprise.

"Rita, would you like us to pray for you?" (I thought, "How embarrassing to be prayed for in front of eighty or ninety strangers, but then maybe it will do some good. It certainly can't do me any harm.")

As I consented I was also secretly thinking it would be nice if there were an Episcopal priest there to pray for me; then I would be sure things would be decent and in order. I was still a bit stuffy about my own denomination.

Just then the leader called, "Father Sherry! Would you come over here and pray for Rita?"

What a quick answer to my inner request! Seeing the warm and loving face of this elderly minister, I relaxed. When Father Sherwood laid his hands on my head and prayed he didn't speak English but spoke fluently in a foreign language! As he prayed, the presence of God broke through to me in such a way that tears of repentance and release began to pour from me, and I realized that he was praying in tongues, in a God-given supernatural language. The power of his prayer, going far beyond his knowledge penetrated into the deep areas of need in my life.

As the joy of the Lord overflowed from my spirit, flooding my mind and body also, a new language began to pour out effortlessly from my lips. *This time it would be a lasting experience.*

---

* The "gift of knowledge" is the opposite of and has nothing to do with the psychic realm! See "The Holy Spirit and You," by Dennis and Rita Bennett, chapter thirteen, for further information.

85

My life in that half hour was absolutely transformed. I knew the world had nothing to offer that could in the slightest compare to this great love and power of God I had experienced, and would go on experiencing.

From that time on my life has been chuck-full of adventure and fulfillment — the way it should have been before. These past fourteen years, to no credit of my own, I have had the opportunity to witness to tens of thousands of people through traveling with my husband, Dennis, to many parts of the world, through radio, television, tapes, and writing. Thank God I received *another chance* and have been allowed to make up for lost time.

Dear friend, right there where you are, won't you, too, start loving God?

RITA (Mrs. Dennis) BENNETT has been active in the charismatic renewal for the past fourteen years, first with her brother, Dr. William Standish Reed, next as assistant to the editor of a widely-read Christian publication and now as the wife of the Rev. Dennis J. Bennett, rector of St. Luke's Episcopal Church in Seattle. Married in 1966, Dennis and Rita have traveled as a team to many parts of the United States, Jamaica, Canada, England and Norway. Dennis Bennett's book, NINE O'CLOCK IN THE MORNING, in addition to telling Dennis' story, also tells how Dennis and Rita met and something of Rita's own testimony. The Bennetts have co-authored a book, THE HOLY SPIRIT AND YOU, a study on living the Spirit-filled life, and Rita has written I'M GLAD YOU ASKED THAT, an Aglow/Logos book dealing with questions women ask about the Christian life and walk.

Adventure Unlimited

By Sister Augustine

During my growing up years I planned many conquests. But whether I was dreaming of becoming an actress, a scientist or a G-woman, travel always was first on my mind.

I did all the things Catholic girls were expected to do at that time. Every Sunday I went to Mass and catechism class. I attended public school because we didn't have a parochial school in my parish. In school I was exposed to the King James Version of the Bible for a few moments each morning . . . and always I longed for those faraway places.

Then, suddenly, I was grown up and it was wartime. I decided to become a nurse. When graduation came my yearning to travel convinced me that the time had come "to join the Navy and see the world."

For the first time in my life I was farther than the Ohio border. I zoomed off to Houston, Texas, for my first Navy duty station. For me it was fun and games with eight hours of nursing duty sandwiched in between. Occasionally I got inside a Catholic church. Occasionally I spoke to the chaplain when he made the rounds. Hangovers were part of life. So were risque jokes and a vocabulary that could shame a stevedore.

Two years later I was assigned to go to flight nurse school with the Air Force in San Antonio, Texas. On that memorable day when the Admiral pinned on my flight nurse wings I was on Cloud #13. To me this milestone in my life spelled the answer to my wildest travel yearnings. I was convinced of this when I received my orders that same day . . . Pearl Harbor, Honolulu, Hawaii, to fly the South Pacific run. Wow! I was so elated I was sure I didn't need a plane to get there. My buoyancy would have carried me to Hawaii and beyond.

It was an excitement that was soon to be shattered. I was on a routine flight to Tokyo, Japan, where I was to spend a month replacing the flight nurse there while she took her vacation. We had passed Wake Island and the point-of-no-return when the plane commander came back to the cabin, looking very solemn. There were 89 men on that flight and me. The plane commander stated in a troubled manner, "I don't know what will be waiting for us when we land in Tokyo. Our country is at war with North Korea."

War! It couldn't be. So soon again? But it was true!

We landed in Tokyo in the midst of chaos. Troops and military police and Japanese civilian police and top brass were everywhere. I didn't find a room and bed for several days. The wounded were already coming in and there was work to do.

My "month" extended into months. To attempt to get away from the sight and smell of death, I tried everything . . . liquor, sex, dope, all on an overseas military base, where there are so few women, everyone knows that you're doing and with whom. One day the Protestant chaplain on the base approached me. We had all been up for several days and nights. Casualties were heavy. He looked into my bloodshot eyes and said gently, "Maybe neither of us likes to be here in this mess, but I suggest we get about doing the Lord's work since He has planted us here."

I was flabbergasted. I had never heard of the Navy being referred to as "the Lord's work." All I wanted to do was to get away from that place . . . far away.

For the first time in my life, I was also seriously in love. Dabney was a Navy pilot assigned to the same squadron as I. He was a soft-spoken Southern Baptist from Atlanta, Georgia.

Returning to California from a flight one April day, I found Dabney's best friend, Sam, at the end of the runway. Sam offered me a ride to the nurses' quarters and when I stopped my chattering long enough, I noted we weren't on the way to the quarters. We were in the military cemetery near San Francisco. Sam stopped the car by a new grave. As I got out of the car, I saw the name on the grave marker. Dabney!

I suppose I got hysterical. I don't remember. It seems that the day my flight had left, Dabney had collapsed in the terminal. They rushed him to the naval hospital in Oakland and discovered he had a brain tumor. He died on the operating table. Dabney was dead and buried before I returned from my flight. Everyone in the squadron had agreed that Sam should be the one to tell me. Sam loved Dabney as much as I did and couldn't bring himself to say those words, "Dabney is dead," so he took me to the graveside to let that mound of earth and marker tell me.

The other nurses were so concerned. They tried to give me a tranquilizer, which I refused. Then they called in the Catholic chaplain. I took one look at the cross on his collar and on his sleeve and literally spit the words at him, "Don't you tell me this is the will of God. And don't give me any of that Jesus bit. Just get out of here!

He understood and left my room.

There were too many memories in San Francisco, so I asked for orders to the East Coast and was assigned to Camp LeJeune, North Carolina. It seemed a hundred isolated miles from nowhere. For diversion, I concentrated on golf.

Everytime I went to tee off I was paired up with a Catholic Navy chaplain, new in the Navy and new on the base. He didn't smoke and he didn't drink anything stronger than ginger ale.

One day we stopped at the 19th hole at a cozy bar just off the fairway. While I sipped my martini, Father Ivers looked squarely at me and asked, "What do you plan to do with the rest of your life?"

In a cocky way I answered, "I plan to be the Navy's first woman admiral."

"I don't think so."

"Well, at least I plan to marry one!"

"No, you won't marry one."

My Yugoslav temper was flaring by this time and I was nasty as I said, "Okay, wise guy, since you seem to have a hot line to the big boss up there, what do you think I'm going to do?"

In an even voice and without ever taking his eyes off mine, Father Ivers answered, "You have great potential if you'll use it. I think you're going to be a nun."

I laughed in his face. "You're out of your mind, man. I could never survive living with all women all the time. And wearing the same kind of outfit everyday. And staying in the same place. No

89

way!" I ordered another martini.

Though I was too muleheaded to realize it at the time, the Lord "arranged" many encounters between Father Ivers and me, in the hospital, socially, on the golf course. Frankly, Father Ivers bothered me. I decided there was only one way to get him out of my hair and that was to confront him with the fact that he was bugging me. I went to his office, knocked on the door, and walked in to be greeted by, "I've been expecting you."

I was completely disarmed by that greeting. I glared at Father Ivers with eyes that said, "I hate your guts. Leave me alone!" He looked at me with eyes that said, "Jesus and I love you."

As I sat there stunned unable to verbalize the litany of complaints I had mentally lined up. Father Ivers reminded me of some of my activities and associations that shouldn't be part of the life of a Christian woman. I felt as though I were living through a *This Is Your Life* show and I wanted to crawl under the desk, but I couldn't move. I wondered who his spy could be. I didn't know then, but I know now. His "spy" was the Holy Spirit who gave him the right words to say to me then, to bring me to my knees.

I can't recall ever before praying for guidance of the Holy Spirit to show me specifically what I was to do with my life. But this day, Father Ivers prayed that prayer for me.

It marked the change that I still cannot explain except to say that God heard that prayer and answered it. Slowly, gradually, little by little, I grew to realize that Father Ivers was right. God did want me to be a nun.

I began investigating all kinds of religious communities, but nothing seemed to jell until I heard about the Glenmary Home Mission Sisters whose work was in rural and small town America. The travel was over and so was the excitement, or so I thought, as I, more surprised than anyone, went off to join the convent.

The adjustment from career woman to nun was unbelievably hard. Yet somehow I got through. After seven years at Glenmary I felt called to a life of deeper prayer. I transferred to a cloistered community in Devon, Pennsylvania, where I remained for four years. I learned much about the church, about Scriptures, about myself. Most important, I knew the love of Jesus, but something in me still felt incomplete. Where was that Christian joy I had heard so much about, but hadn't experienced? Where was the problem . . . in me or in my religious community or both?

Yet, despite my restlessness, the Holy Spirit was very much at work in me. During this interim in my life I met a Mercy Sister who was a nurse and psychologist. Every time I met her I marveled at her serenity and joy. One day I just blurted it out . . . "Sister Jean, you've been a nun as long as I have. What do you have that makes you different?"

With a joyful radiance she answered, "I have the Lord."

"Do you mean that after I've been in the convent thirteen years I don't have Him?"

"You don't have Him in the same way, my sister. Open your heart and invite Him in."

No formula. No strategic blueprint. No set of rules. It sounded too simple and good to be real. But when I got back to the cloister that evening I prayed the simplest prayer of my whole life. "Jesus . . . come into my heart and take over my life."

As the days went on, I was overcome with a powerful restlessness. I conferred with my spiritual director, and after some months, he and my religious superiors concurred that the Lord was calling me back to the active religious life. In time I returned to my home in Pennsylvania to get myself collected and seek the Lord's will for the future.

On the very day I got home, Vera, a dear friend from my secretarial days, called to invite me to join her at a Full Gospel Businessmen's Fellowship meeting. I had never heard of the group but I wanted to see Vera so much I agreed to go. It was a lively meeting and I felt led to ask for the baptism in the Holy Spirit. I was prayed over that night and at several subsequent meetings. Glorious things happened all around me, but nothing seemed to change in me. I was puzzled, discouraged, frustrated.

Several months later, Vera invited me to attend an ecumenical service in her church, St. Martin's Episcopal, in Monroeville, Pennsylvania.

That night during the prayer and praise service, a Presbyterian minister gave his testimony. He, too, had been older when he entered the ministry and I could identify with his frustrations in the seminary with much younger members in the same class and the search for Christian joy he found so lacking. He gave an altar call at the end of his testimony but I sat immobile. The devil had moved in, and I refused to budge. "Lord," I prayed, "I'm not moving. I've asked for the baptism so many times and nothing ever happens. I'm not moving."

Like a neon sign, the words from Mark 11:24 flashed before me . . . *"Everything you ask and pray for, believe that you have it already, and it will be yours."* I still couldn't move but I did pray in my way, "Lord, this is the last time I'm asking. I want the baptism, and I want it right now."

As though some physical force took hold of the back of my blouse, I felt myself get up from the pew and walk forward to the altar. I told those praying, "I want the baptism in the Holy Spirit and I want it right now."

After a few preliminary questions to make certain if I understood what I was asking for and its scriptural background, and if I had forgiveness in my heart, they began to pray over me. It was at that moment the Lord revealed to me why I hadn't received before . . . because I had studied seven languages and I didn't believe the Lord could give me a new one! But, in that wondrous moment, I began to pray in a NEW language.

I don't know if it's proper to dance in the Episcopal church, but that night I danced. And I've been dancing, inside and out ever since. That night of wonder and peace and joy was January 19, 1971.

In April, 1971, I returned to the Glenmary Sisters to share in their ministry. Shortly after that I was prayed over at a prayer meeting and this prophecy was given: "My daughter, you will travel many places for Me and some of them will be the desert. This is only the beginning."

Truly, it is a beginning of a new and incredible adventure . . . adventure unlimited and unpredictable in the Lord's ministry. Praise God!

SISTER GUS is a Catholic evangelist with a diverse background. She is a native of Greensburg, Pennsylvania. For the past four years, she has been involved in full-time youth ministry, teen-age retreats and Scripture classes. She has recently completed a book about youth ministry among teen-agers, entitled THE NEW CHILDREN, published by Whitaker House in Monroeville, Pennsylvania. Sister Gus has been active in Women's Aglow for the past two years and is Spiritual Life chairman for the Greensburg Women's Aglow Fellowship.